SHEILA SPENCE

PICTURES OF ME

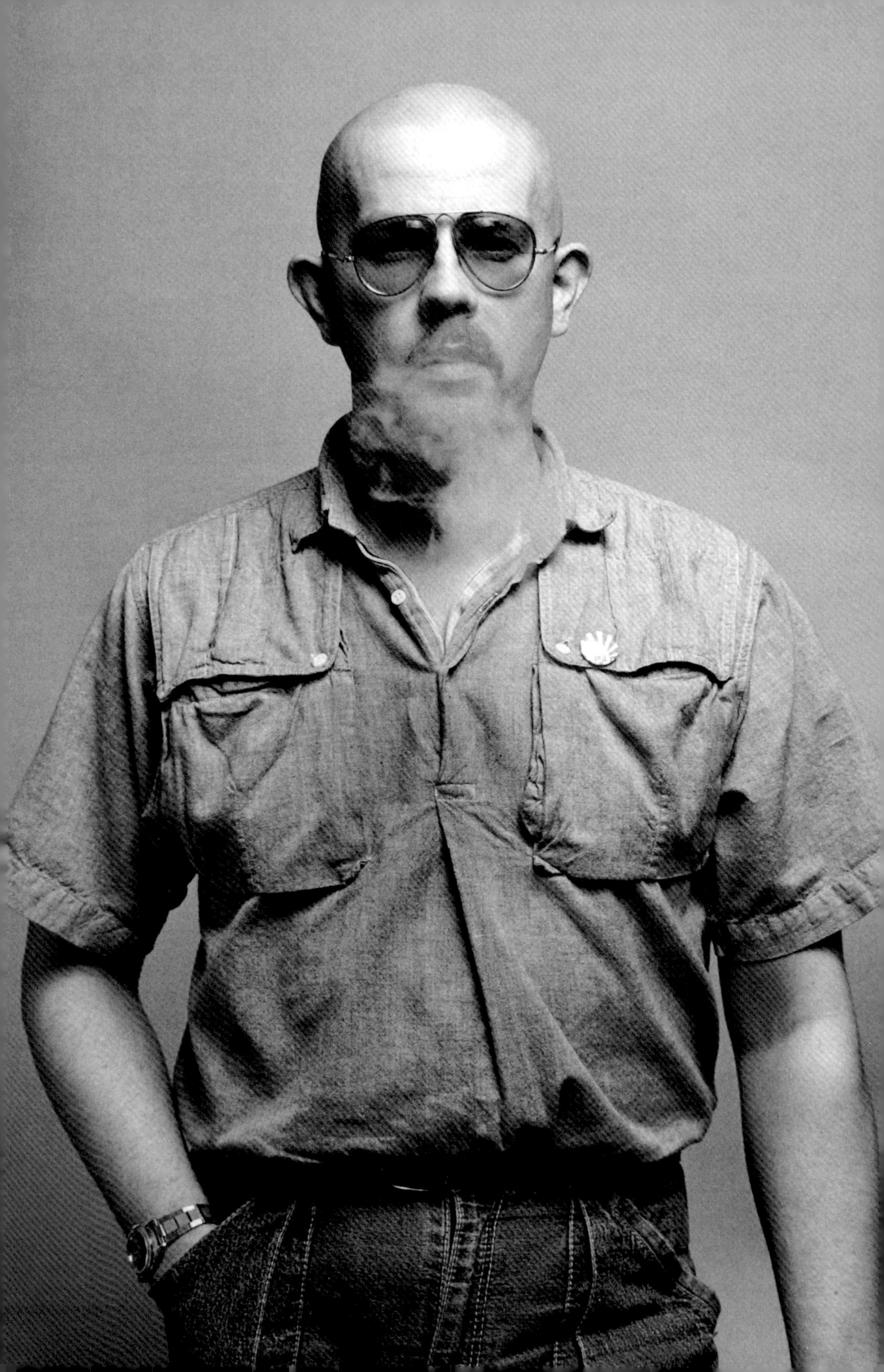

SHEILA SPENCE

PICTURES OF ME

Curated by
Mary Reid

Essay by
Mary Reid

Interview by
Robert McKaskell

Organized by
The Winnipeg Art Gallery

THE WINNIPEG ART GALLERY

November 8, 2008–February 15, 2009

2. *Roderick*, 1985

THE WINNIPEG ART GALLERY

Library and Archives Canada Cataloguing in Publication

Reid, Mary, 1972-

Sheila Spence : pictures of me : the Winnipeg Art Gallery, November 8, 2008-February 15, 2009 / curated by Mary Reid ; interview by Robert McKaskell ; essay by Mary Reid.

Includes bibliographical references.

ISBN 978-0-88915-002-7

1. Spence, Sheila, 1952- --Exhibitions. 2. Photography, Artistic-- Exhibitions.
I. McKaskell, Robert, 1943- II. Winnipeg Art Gallery III. Title. IV. Title: Pictures of me.

TR647.S697 2008 779.092 C2008-906351-1

Credits

CURATOR Mary Reid, Curator, Contemporary Art and Photography, The Winnipeg Art Gallery

EDITOR Heidi Harms

PROOFREADER Heather Mousseau, The Winnipeg Art Gallery

DESIGNER Lisa Friesen, The Winnipeg Art Gallery

PRINTER Friesens Corporation, Altona, Manitoba

DISTRIBUTION ABC Art Books Canada Distribution, www.ABCartbookscanada.com

Printed in Canada.

Supported by the Canada Council for the Arts, the Manitoba Arts Council,
the Imperial Tobacco Canada Foundation and the W.H. & S.E. Loewen Foundation Inc.

Media Sponsor: Winnipeg Free Press

Canada Council for the Arts Conseil des Arts du Canada

Manitoba Arts Council / Conseil des arts du Manitoba

The Free Press
We're there for you

CONTENTS

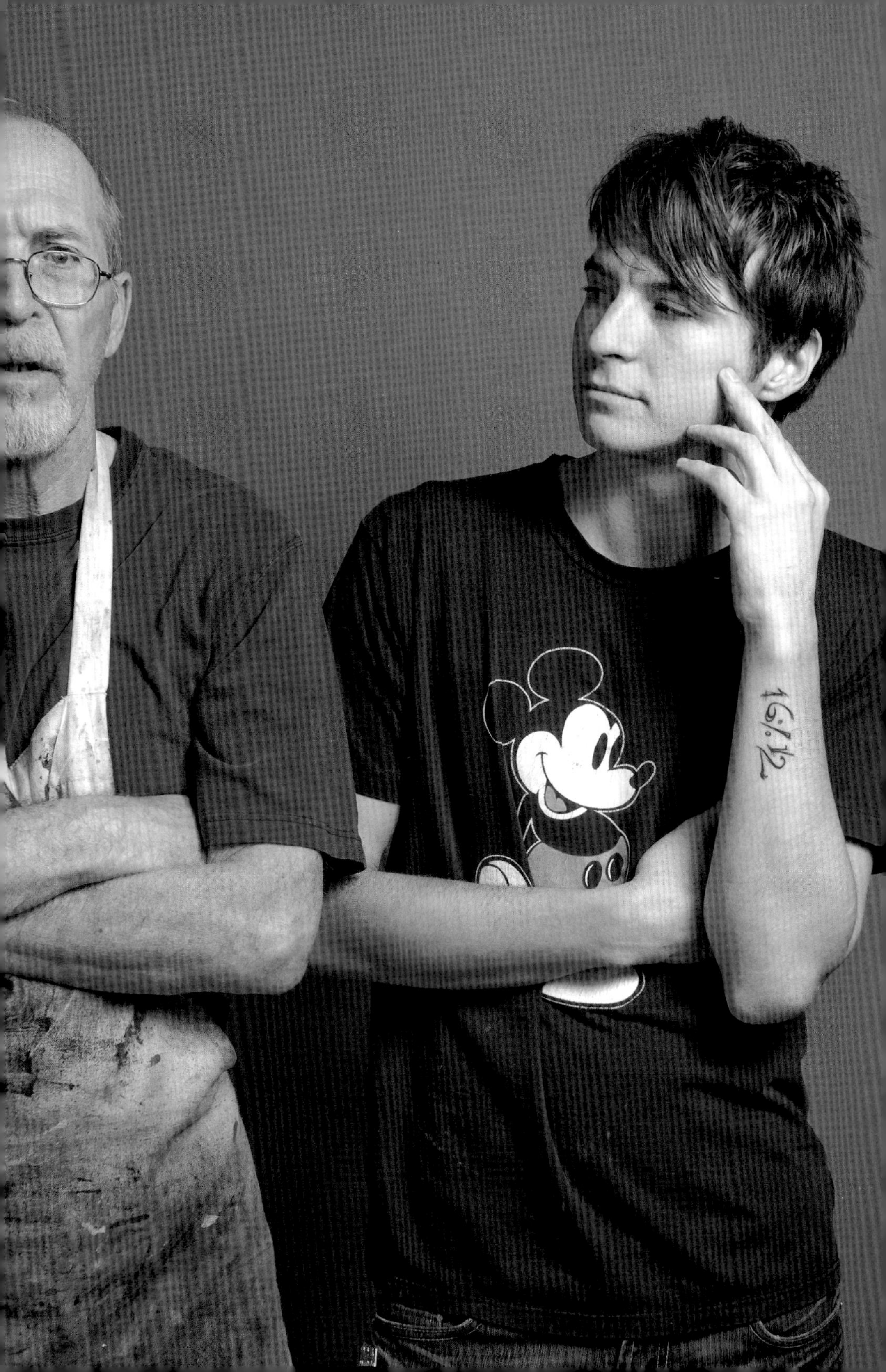

FOREWORD

Stephen D. Borys, Ph.D. Director, The Winnipeg Art Gallery

For well over twenty-five years, Winnipeg artist Sheila Spence has entrenched herself in the practice of photographing people—portraits, more specifically. *Pictures of Me* is a survey of Spence's artistic career highlighting her most well-known and critically recognized bodies of work. However, the entire thesis of the exhibition and catalogue essay, written by WAG curator Mary Reid, resides in the understanding that every picture Spence takes is in fact another representation of herself. With a sensitive, subtle approach, she has created not only a collective self-portrait; she has produced a remarkable perspective on her immediate community.

Sheila Spence worked as a staff photographer for sixteen years at The Winnipeg Art Gallery and during that time Gallery policy prevented us from exhibiting her work. Her work was shown as part of *A Sense of Place: Photography in Manitoba* at the WAG in 1986. The following year, the Gallery purchased *Untitled [Portrait of a Male]*, *Nora Smoking* and *Jenny*, and *Gerry* was donated to the permanent collection. In 2007 the WAG acquired five more works by Spence, including two photographs donated by the artist, rounding out the representation of her work in the permanent collection.

70. *Keith and Eric*, 2008 (1 of 2 components)

Firstly, I would like to express my gratitude to the artist, Sheila Spence, for her dedication to the exhibition and catalogue. This project celebrates her art-making and her longstanding ties to the WAG and its staff. I am grateful to Mary Reid for her management and contributions at all stages of the exhibition, including her enlightening and erudite essay in the catalogue. My appreciation goes to Robert McKaskell, former WAG Academic Curator, for his insightful handling of the interview with the artist. As well, editor Heidi Harms and WAG designer Lisa Friesen are to be commended for their fine work on this publication. I commend all of these individuals along with the entire staff of the WAG for their hard work in bringing this exhibition to fruition.

Thanks must go to The University of Winnipeg, Investors Group, the Manitoba Arts Council, and the Art Gallery of Southwestern Manitoba, as well as a private collector, for their generous loans to the exhibition. We also acknowledge the support of the Canada Council for the Arts through its Assistance to Art Museums and Public Galleries program, the Manitoba Arts Council, the Imperial Tobacco Canada Foundation, and the W.H. & S.E. Loewen Foundation. The Winnipeg Free Press also provided valuable support through its media sponsorship. All of these organizations help us to continue presenting high calibre exhibitions, like *Sheila Spence: Pictures of Me*, to our audiences.

44. *Ratt Brothers, West Broadway*, 1997

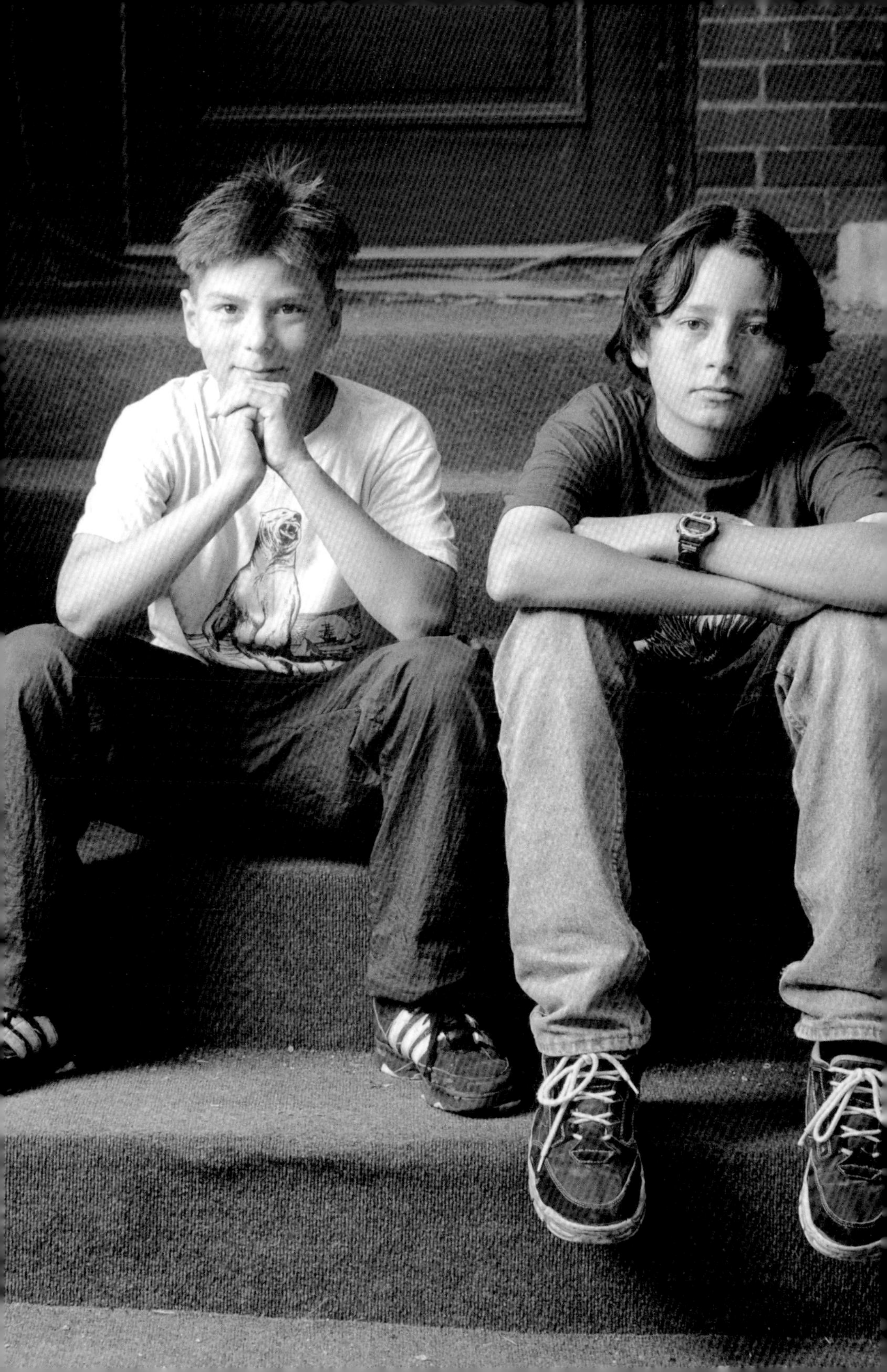

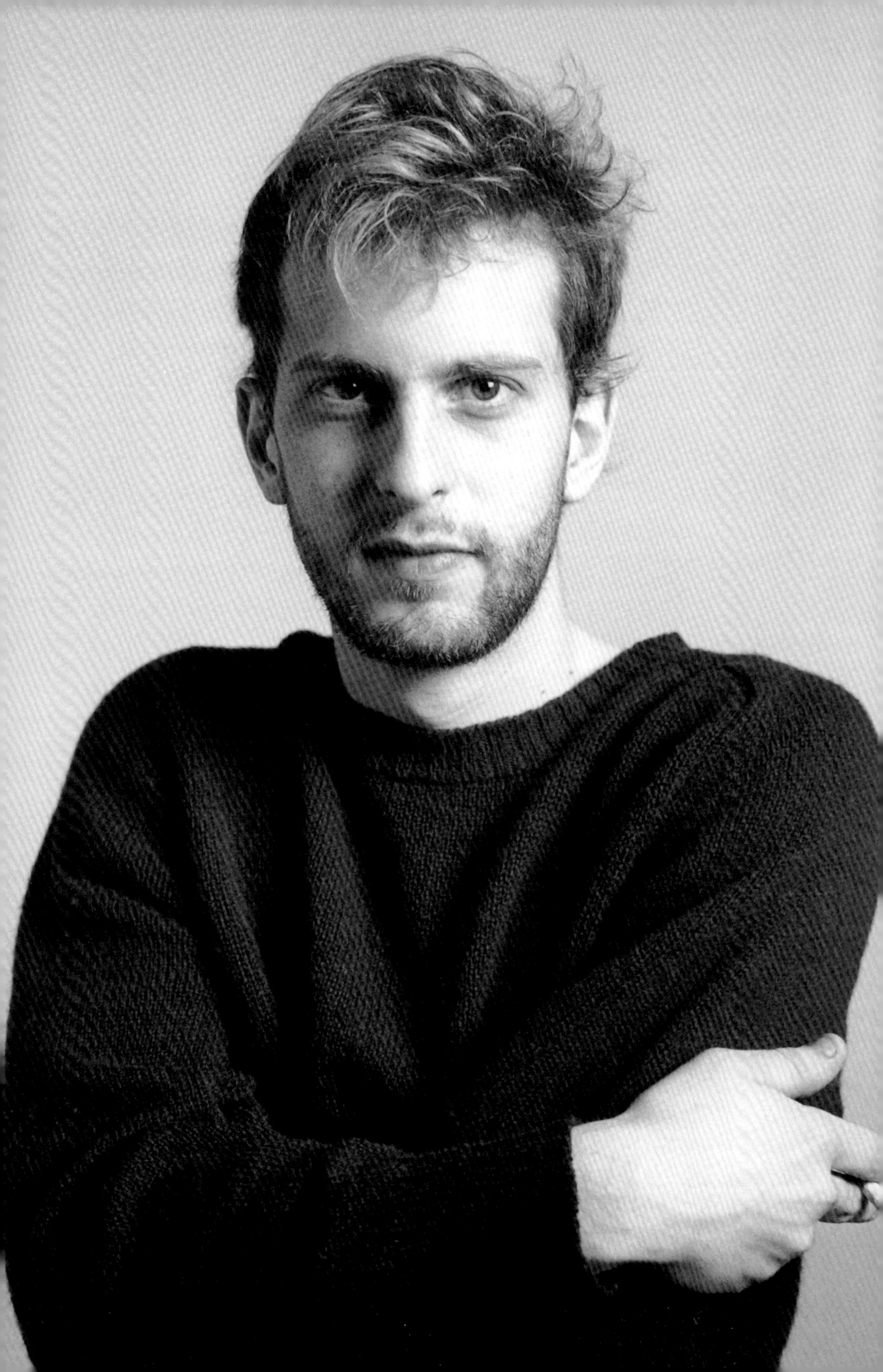

THE MANY FACES OF SHEILA SPENCE

Mary Reid

"Portraiture shows us who we are and how we feel about who we are..."[1]

Sheila Spence has dedicated her creative practice to the exploration of portrait photography, investigating complexities that embody personal relationships, the constructions and contradictions of identity, and notions of community. In many ways her work over the last 25 years has been dedicated to her own search regarding her place in the community and family that surround her.

When I first saw Spence's photographs, I was instantly drawn to the faces, all sorts of faces: male, female, children, adults, young, old, happy, sad, introspective, guarded, open... What is it that distinguishes one person from the other? Their dress, their appearance, their characteristics, their relationship to the photographer? Spence's subjects are drawn from her circle of friends, her immediate family, and her Winnipeg community of neighbours, acquaintances, artists, cultural workers, and partners.

In our contemporary existence, pictures of people's faces are probably the most common type of images that we encounter on a day-to-day basis. "We all carry at least one photo-ID in our wallet."[2] However, Spence is

4. *Untitled [Portrait of a Male]*, 1986

not merely taking snapshots of faces. Her body of work is well entrenched in the genre and tradition of formal portraiture. Compositionally sound, exquisitely lit, and meticulously printed, her black and white portraits act as a foil for the representation of more complex ideas. Spence's images are a "culmination of the modern artistic interest in the individual."[3] In all cases Spence is not just taking a picture; she is capturing a psychological relationship between the people present, between herself and the subject, and between that person and his/her own persona/psyche. In a single critical frame Spence captures fleeting expressions, and it is in this "seizure of a single illuminating moment in time in which the essence of the sitter's identity is captured."[4] Spence not only captures how her subjects present themselves, her work delivers to us an intimate self-portrait of the artist. Every photograph offers multiple layers of insight into the artist and her subject. Seen collectively, these portraits can be considered representing the same face—the face of the photographer, the face of Spence herself.

Photographic portraiture elicits an unusual experience in the viewer. "The portrait is always an active site of human relationships and interactions."[5] Unlike an abstract painting or sculpture, photography, because of its perceived faithful representation and ubiquitous presence in our daily life, provides the potential opportunity for viewers to forget they are looking at a work of art. Almost unconsciously there is a desire on the part of the viewer to completely remove this layer of understanding, this filter of presentation, this act of the artist, in an effort to connect directly with the person being depicted.[6] Doubling as "windows through which we glimpse at lives lived; portraiture elicits the power of empathy, activating our curiosity and understanding of another person."[7] This experience can occur even if the portrait itself is staged. It is the willingness of the viewer to almost disregard the actual process of the artist that provides this unique and at times ironic characteristic of photographic portraits.

Part of the energy of Spence's work lies in the very act of looking, through which she draws attention to the power relations held in the gaze itself: the photographer's, the spectator's, and the subject's.[8] Spence cleverly subverts the traditional authoritative role of the photographer. Despite the control an artist can assert while in the studio, Spence is clearly more concerned with the quality of what the sitter brings to the session. Part listener, part conversationalist, part confidante, Spence in her manner weaves around her subjects in order to draw this quality out further. Many times a session will not be successful. Her subject will be too conscious of posing for the camera, too aware that a doubling is taking place. Hence in Spence's work power lies with both the subject and the artist who is creating an object. This is a much different challenge than that of an artist working in another medium, yet Spence embraces this tipping of the scales, this equal tension of control and lack of control, and boldly confronts the spectator to continue this act of looking, with the inherent dominance that the gaze contains.

This act of looking was first explored by Spence during the mid-1980s, in her first major body of work focusing on individual portraits.[9] With the subjects photographed from the waist up and positioned in front of a neutral background, the portraits are devoid of a recognizable sense of place or time. Spence's portraits are of people who are aware they are being photographed. They are conscious of the act taking place and as a consequence they seem poised but not necessarily posed. Although they may have been instructed by Spence "to be yourself, to act natural, to forget about the camera," "it is impossible to rid oneself of all fabrication. Self-exposure goes hand in hand with makeup, clothing and mannerisms."[10] Undoubtedly Spence's subjects all hold a general notion of what they look like and they try to project this onto the camera. However, the person portrayed and the portrait are two entirely different things.[11] Many of Spence's subjects were likely surprised when faced with a representation of how they in fact looked.[12] Perhaps this is because we all spend less time looking at ourselves than others do, or because when we do look at ourselves in a mirror it is the reverse of what is depicted in a photographed

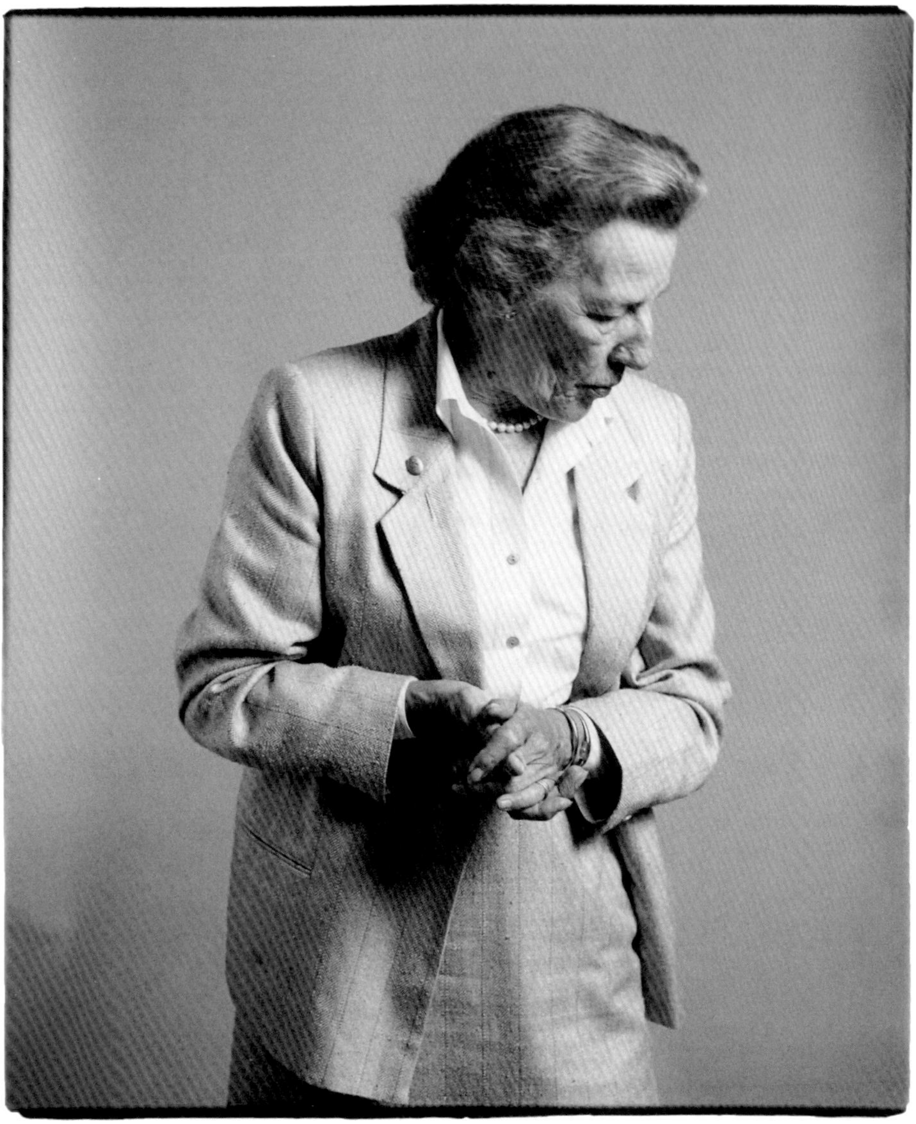

3. *Gerry*, 1985

portrait. It is Spence's ability to capture an expression on her subject's face that reveals the truths of their character and personalities.

In *Untitled [Portrait of a Male]* (1986), the subject, a nice-looking young man, looks directly at the viewer/photographer with a slightly cross-eyed stare. Sporting a head of curly locks and a close-shaven beard, he hugs himself, which gives him an appearance of vulnerability. The sweater he wears is almost too big for him, and the apparent lack of an undergarment makes me think it might be a bit itchy, yet he presses it against himself, either in an effort to protect or distract himself. At the same time, he is grasping a lit and partially smoked cigarette between his nail-bitten fingers. The side lighting intensifies the contrast of the loose dark sweater against his white neck and the slightly revealed top of his shoulder, further supporting the fragile quality imbedded in this representation. Yet there is also a defiance, an "I couldn't care less" attitude, that again may be a means of self-protection and preservation or even an indication that he is not a completely willing participant in this interaction.

The wonderful thing about people is that they remind you of other people. Although I do not know the person depicted in this portrait, the pose, the attitude, the vulnerability, even the man's hair and clothing remind me of a good friend of mine and so I, the viewer, inject all my thoughts and feelings about the person I know into my understanding and reading of this work. Because I care for my friend, enjoy his company, and even miss him, I begin to establish an intimate connection with the man depicted in this work, a man I have never met, yet feel some closeness towards.

Another exceptional work in this series is *Gerry* (1985). Presented here is an obviously aging woman, sporting an understated yet smart, well-tailored suit and the requisite string of pearls. Compared to *Untitled [Portrait of a Male]* the lighting is softer, the contrasts more subtle, the field of vision expanded slightly. Gerry looks down, and subverts the camera; she does not engage in the gaze. The focus instead turns to her well-manicured clasped hands. Perhaps an unconscious gesture, it evokes grace and elegance. My reading of this portrait is much different than of *Untitled [Portrait of a Male]*. There is a quiet aspect about this work, but certainly no weakness. I get the impression that Gerry is a strong woman, who is neither shy nor uninterested in having her picture taken; she is simply comfortable in her own skin and possesses a form of inner strength that is not overt, yet is definitely palpable. Perhaps her decision to look away comes from that position.[13]

It is important to remember when looking at these works dating from the 1980s, that the moment depicted is well past and yet the subject of the picture "addresses his/herself for the camera in the present and for the unknown context of the future."[14] This perpetual potential for the object, the photograph, and by consequence the subject it depicts, to remain forever in the present, tweaks at an intimacy with the viewer that is never quite fully realized.[15] The man and woman in the photographs discussed previously have aged, and in the case of Gerry, have since passed away, yet their presence is with us in the here and now, just as the memory of them resides in Spence's mind. So, as objects, they document Spence's experience and understanding of these people, which in turn is a reflection of Spence herself back to us, the viewer. They also become objects that spark the viewer's memory of that person, of that time, or even of a different person they remember.

By the end of 1980s, Spence had moved away from doing individual portraits and towards creating family portraits. Twenty years have passed, and in 2007, Spence returned to further explore the subject matter of the individual portrait. Now the works are produced digitally and on a much larger scale. In these new works she produces a less romanticized vision of her subjects. The subject's face dominates the entire frame of the composition with a gaze posed directly at the photographer and viewer. The extreme close-ups give the images a tension of immediacy yet create an uncomfortable aversion to scale. Almost monstrous faces or disembodied gods, these large heads produce a sensation of both emotional familiarity and detachment in the viewer. The eyes hold one's attention "as they appear to look out beyond the immediate surrounding to embrace a vision of something not yet fabricated into existence."[16]

Given his age, his smirk, slightly tattered top, and freckled cheeks and nose, *Parker* (2007) embodies the future, even perhaps a collective hope for the future. Spence's investigation into this subject matter again is similar, although some of the variables have changed, such as the equipment, the printing process, and, more profoundly, the subjects themselves, as well as the photographer herself. Everyone has aged, new people have come into her life, others have left, some have been born, and others have died. This new body of work is starker in appearance, almost too real, and perhaps a bit unforgiving. It is a representation of her life at this moment in time, as a photographer and as a person.

Many visitors to this exhibition at The Winnipeg Art Gallery will know the people presented in Spence's work; however, many more will not. She offers us portraits of her Winnipeg community. Taken in a contemporaneous context, Spence's work fits well with the media's obsession with presenting its viewing public with "reality TV" shows. The recent general population's mass interest in "real people" (no matter how fake their façade is) comes to bear on the current perception and presentation of Spence's work. Spence has always been interested in "real people," those who have no desire to have their lives scripted and performed to a sizable, anonymous audience. Through the exhibition of these portraits, Spence's subjects are elevated in significance, to become, for a period, highly recognizable. What is the effect of this action? Will an image of Nora be remembered when someone bumps into her at a community event; will a person unknown to Calvin approach him on the street in a haze of "I think I know you"? Or, after seeing the exhibition, will visitors feel more as if they had just flipped through someone's family album, recognizing some people, tracing continuities, resemblances, narratives, and relationships with some active,

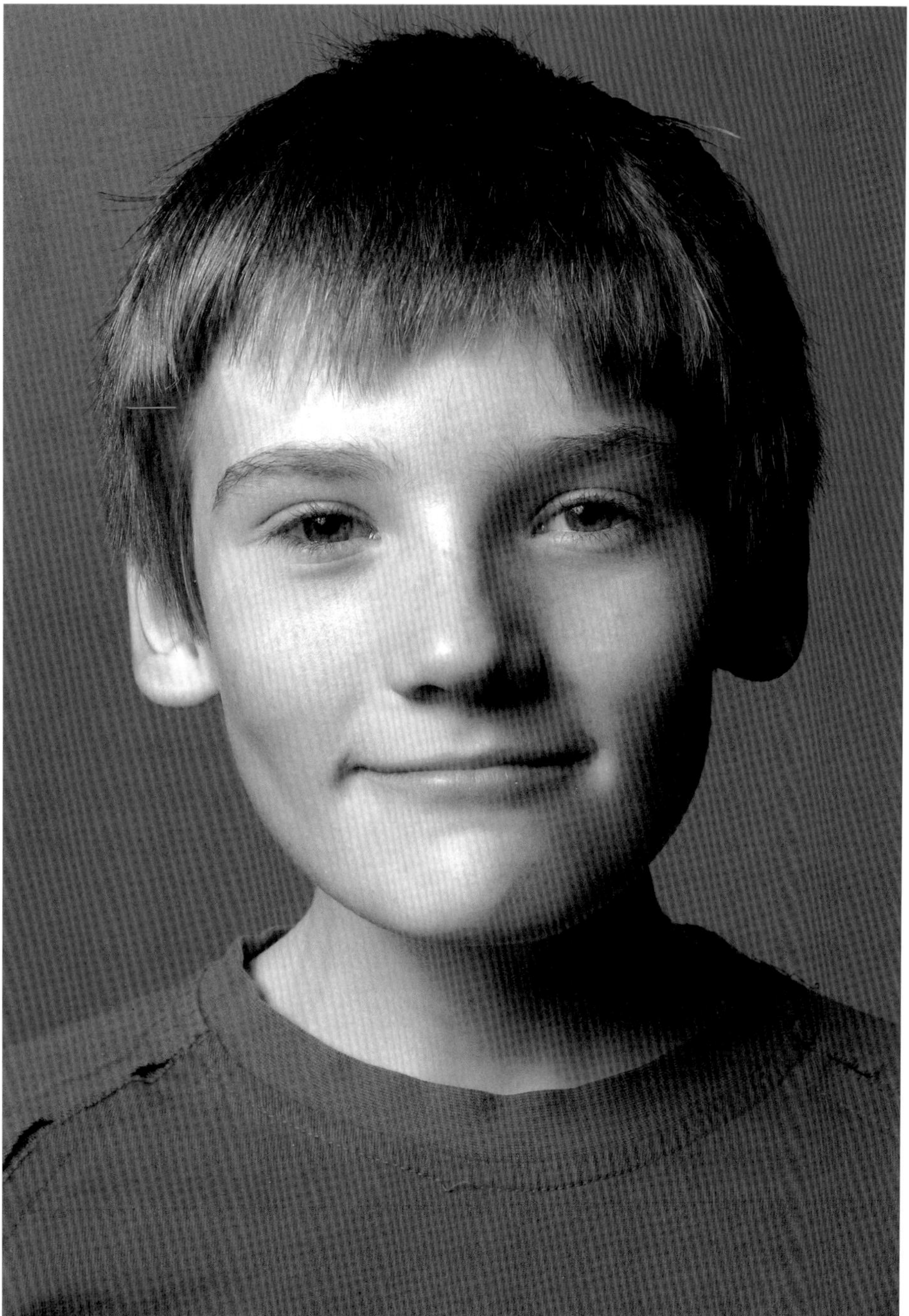

55. *Parker*, 2007

albeit latent or hidden, curiosity? We all have families, and how they operate is usually a mystery to those both inside and outside the circle. When looking at someone else's family album, I am always looking for clues to understanding their family that in turn might give me some insight into my own.

Spence's second major body of work dealt with just that—families; in particular, investigating people's place within their families. Through the capturing of body language, these works reveal the assumed and (self-) imposed individual roles of family members from both a physical and emotional standpoint. One piece consists of multiple images, with each image focused on a separate family member. To compose a "family portrait" in this manner further magnifies and interrogates the relationships, tensions, and ties that bind people together. All of the images show a sense of intimacy between the subjects and the photographer, displaying a sense of trust and comfort that is akin to looking into a mirror. With incredible subtlety, Spence's images reflect the complexity and high emotive weight relationships play in our individual lives. She creates a family album in which conventional and unconventional social roles and rituals are played out in the same space.

Typically, the formal family portrait as we expect it to be depicts the "perfect" nuclear familial unit, normally documenting significant moments in people's lives.[17] I know that my family is not perfect, but why do I want that perception represented in a family portrait? Spence's results yield a conflicting critique on the notion of family. Her subjects put forward their idealized perceptions of their selves, while through her lens Spence mines the connections and disconnects that are part of every family, every relationship.

In many ways Spence deconstructs the family unit. This postmodern urge to unpack, break apart, and analyze is deeply rooted in feminist theory.[18] This impulse is not a coincidence, as Spence's perspective has been profoundly shaped by feminism and activism for the past 25 years.

Between 1991 and 1995, Spence was part of the artist collective Average Good Looks, a group that created works for the public domain to stimulate discourse on lesbian and gay rights. One example was a billboard in Osborne Village that questioned the definition of family with shots of couples and individuals arranged above the statement: "gays & lesbians. your family."

The four-part work *Bernadette, Jude, and Katherine* (1988) presents a non-traditional sense of family, a family of friends, and/or sisters, and/or lovers. Photographed in natural light against a brick wall of what is presumably a house, the one I conjecture they all share, the women are casual and somewhat similar in their dress. It is often thought that people are drawn to other people who are similar to themselves; hence it is not surprising that Bernadette, Jude, and Katherine share a physical resemblance in their clothing, hairstyles, and even eyeglasses. In the work itself, the emotions projected range from sadness to laughter, supported by an underlying tenderness. Looking at this piece, it is evident that

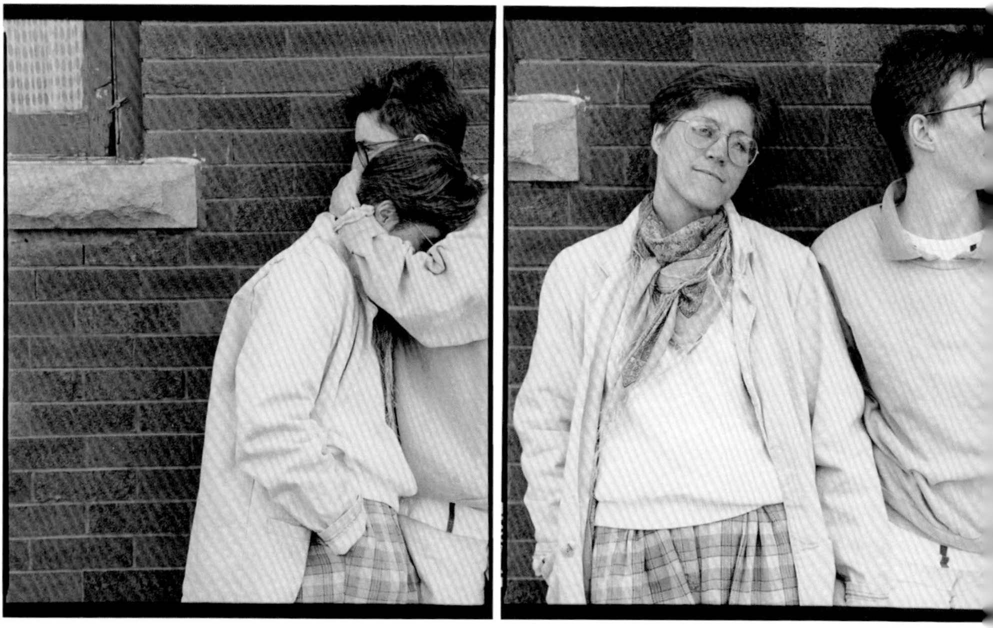

19. *Bernadette, Jude, and Katherine*, 1988

Jude is the connector. She has the ability to keep this family together or separated. My looking also prompts a concern for what is bothering Bernadette. Jude hugs her in comfort and yet afterwards Bernadette stares off into the distance, seemingly disconnected from what is taking place. At the same time I am curious to know what Katherine is saying that causes an outburst of giggles between her and Jude. I want to be in on the joke. I want to share in the drama and comedy that make up this family.

Sheila Spence has since returned to the *Families* series, not only to document a "follow-up" in the lives of her first set of subjects, but to further her introspective trajectory of how one changes, shifts, and adjusts to belonging and being a part of something larger (that is perhaps not always by choice). The works *Sharon and Bob* (1988) and *Kim and Sharon* (2007) exemplify this investigation. In the 1988 piece both subjects seem somewhat unhappy and there is a perceived disconnect between the two. The two people are "holding on," and I don't mean just around the waist. In

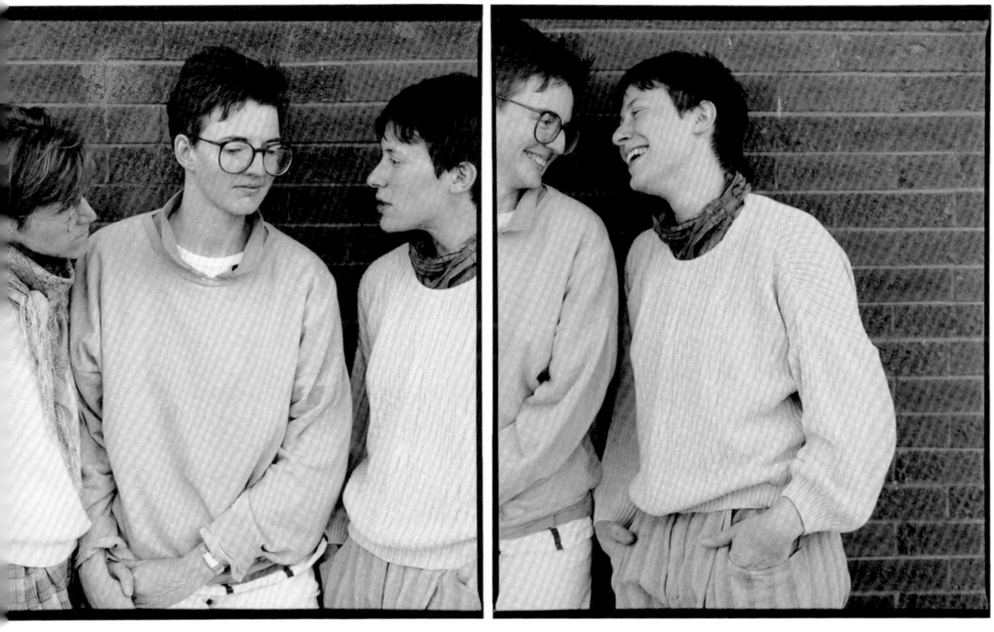

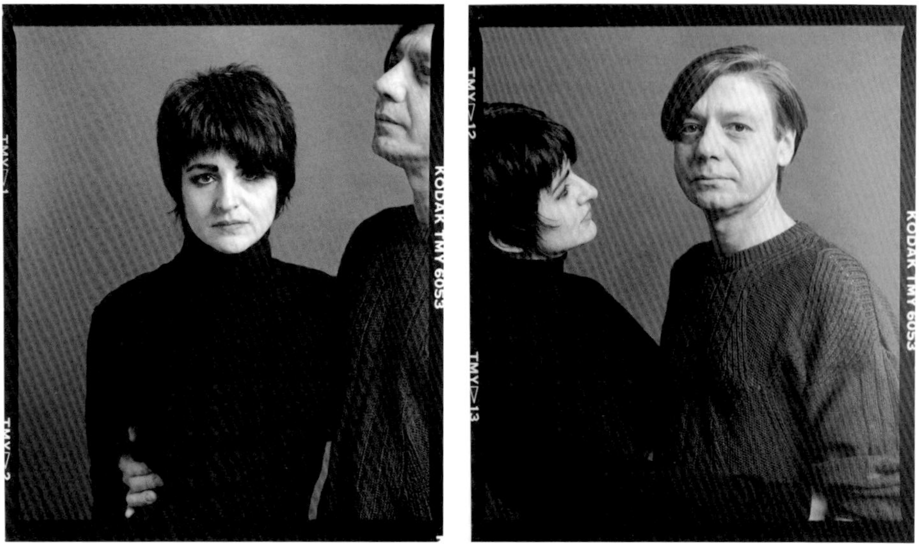

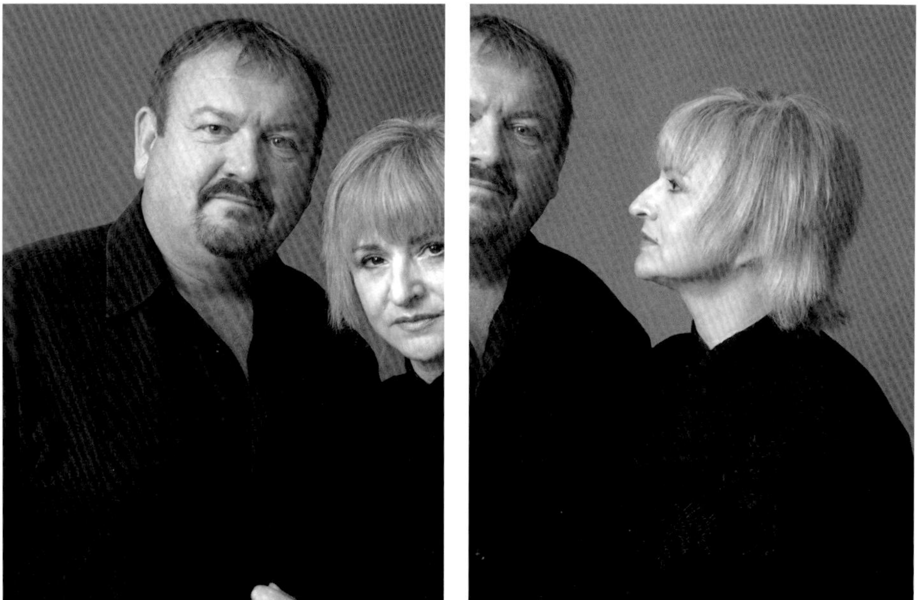

Above 20. *Sharon and Bob*, 1988
Below 61. *Kim and Sharon*, 2007

the 2007 work Sharon reappears, but with a different partner. The strong connection between this new couple is palpable. The need to possess has been replaced with a sense of comfortable belonging.

Family portraiture in Spence's hand is a conceptual act commenting on larger issues of personal identity, both hers and that of her subjects, as well as close familial and romantic relationships, and social inequalities.[19] Given the focus contemporary media places on exploiting and sensationalizing personal pain and anguish, along with the joy and elation brought about by romantic and familial relationships, Spence's interrogation of this subject matter is highly relevant in today's context. Yet this is not what drives Spence's desire to produce this body of work. It is important to note that Spence began looking at the family unit in the late 1980s, at a time of excessiveness and adoption of political correctness. Traditional modes of understanding families had already been in question for some time; however, gay and lesbian issues, along with the inequalities of women in the workforce, were at the forefront of societal politics at that time. Through her exploration of what could be considered "sacred" territory, Spence adds to the debate of what a family can be, while at the same time researching her own place within hers. Her "follow-up" adds to this argument. Many of the issues have progressed more positively since that time, but there is still a long way to go before social equality is achieved. In her later portraits of family, the viewer can document what has changed, and wonder what will come next, perhaps even expecting the unexpected.

There is a famous quote by American painter John Singer Sargent: "Every time I paint a portrait, I lose a friend." This is not normally the case with Spence, as many of her subjects have remained friends with her for a lifetime, and yet this did happen with the West Broadway series. In the late 1990s, Spence completed a body of work titled *Portraits of a Neighbourhood: Images of West Broadway*. Using her camera as a wedge into her community, one of the toughest in Winnipeg, Spence documented the young children and teenagers who resided in her neighbourhood.

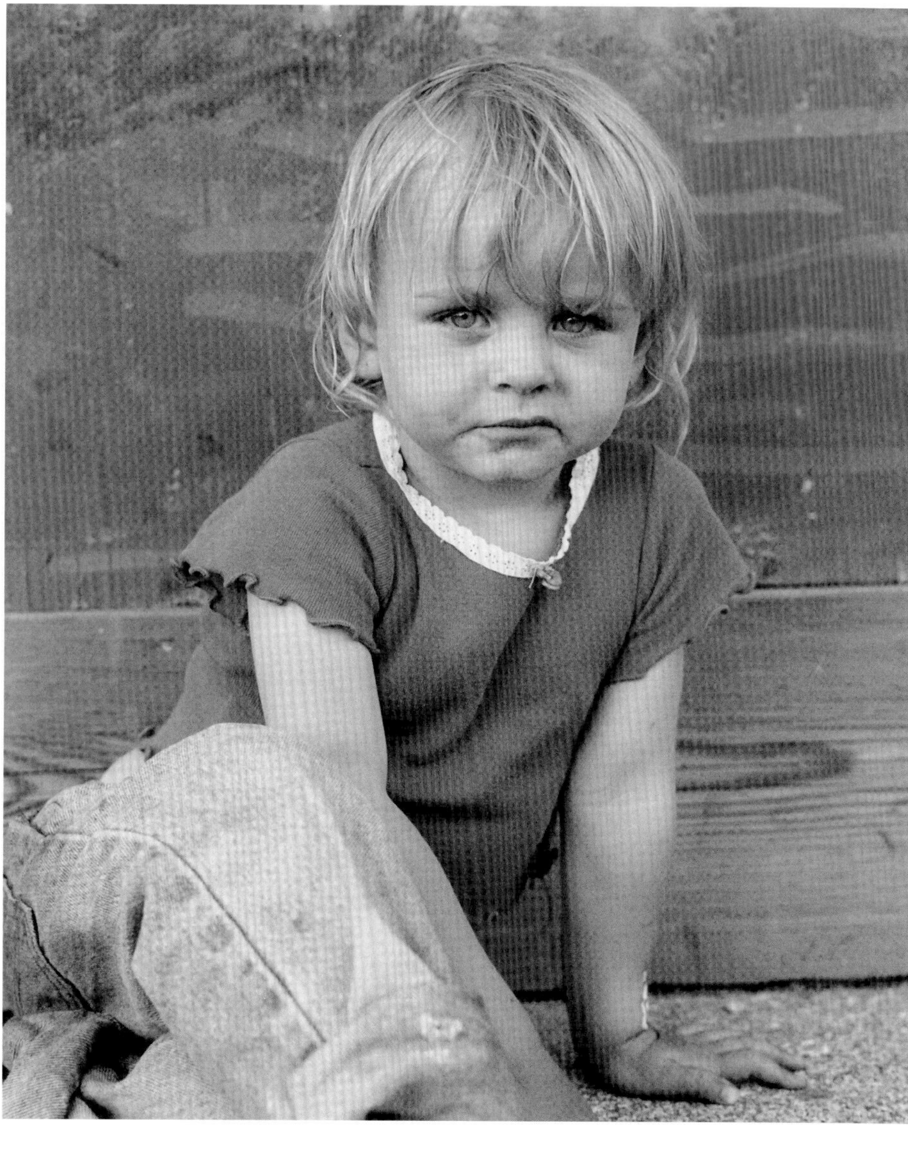

40. *Stephanie, West Broadway*, 1997

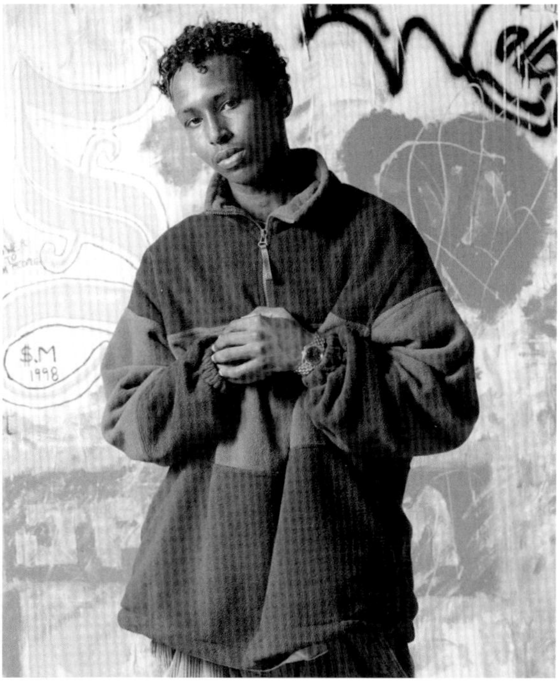

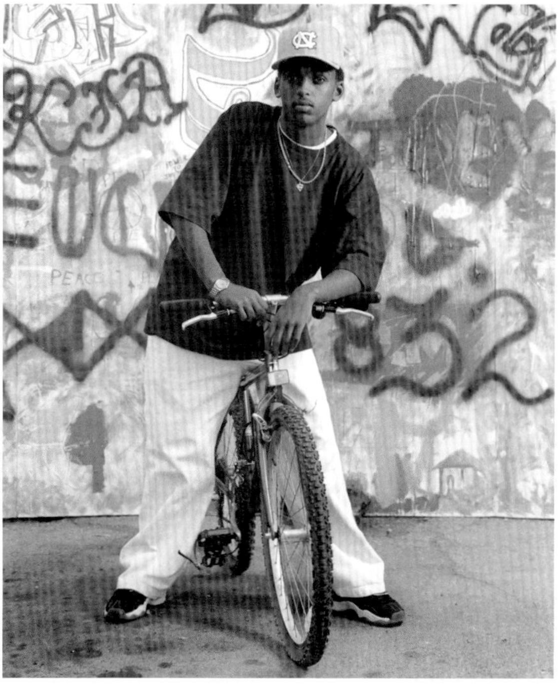

Above 45. *Boy with Wristwatch, West Broadway*, 1998
Below 51. *Superman, West Broadway*, 1998

Through the taking of their portraits, Spence developed a trust and a relationship with members of her community towards whom she initially held some hesitation.

Nucking Futs, West Broadway (1998) and *Eight, Tray, Deuce, West Broadway* (1998) are two of the most visually arresting images in this series. Set against a graffiti-covered wall, her subjects stare with tremendous force and anger into the camera. Posing with gang signs, and even sporting gang insignias on ball caps, these young people look as if they could have come right out of a rap music video. Their bravura is in opposition to the undercurrent of insecurity evident on their faces. This may be because "[t]he will to show oneself is also a wish to see someone looking at me and to have one's own existence confirmed."[20] The three-year-old girl in *Stephanie* (1997) embodies this desire more profoundly than any of the teenagers presented. Her dirty, sombre, little face meets the camera with eyes full of experience that perhaps she does not quite understand, yet is her reality.

Once again, Spence did not instruct her subjects how to pose, nor did she take the picture of anyone who was not willing.[21] Once the works were printed she would return and share copies of the photographs with her subjects, further strengthening her bond with them.[22] Collectively, these images are a powerful look at the representation of youth, notions of community, civic pride, and social stereotyping. Although exhibited and reproduced on several occasions, it was an exhibition of this body of work in 1999 at Gallery 1C03, University of Winnipeg, that resulted in a controversy brutally played out in the local media and in the gallery itself. During the opening of the exhibition, parents were vocally defensive about the portrayal of their children as gang members.[23] Some of the subjects themselves questioned the ownership of the artworks, while politicians and community activists debated the issues of West Broadway being labelled "murder's half acre."[24] The works in question were literally removed from the gallery walls during the opening reception.[25] Throughout this process

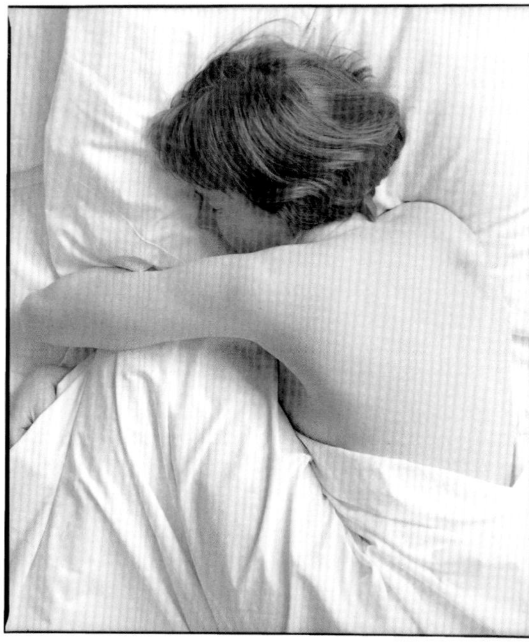

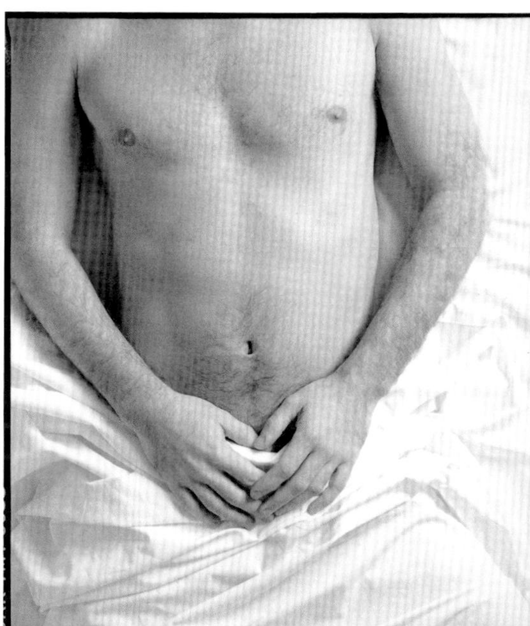

Above 33. *See Whose Face it Wears [#15]*, 1989-90
Below 32. *See Whose Face it Wears [#14]*, 1989-90

Spence learned a lot about herself, her community, and her relationships to people. As objects, this series represents a very difficult period in her life, yet it also signifies her willingness as an artist to understand herself through her environment. Instead of shying away, she embraced where she was living and became an integral part of that neighbourhood.

Spence has produced other bodies of work that are also represented in the current exhibition. During a residency at the Banff Centre for Fine Arts in 1989, she completed the series *See Whose Face it Wears*, a set of landscape-type portraits of people enveloped in white sheets, seemingly asleep. These evocative images take advantage of the contrast between the human body and the sculptural form of the sheets. They also begin to shift the balance of power to the viewer. Instead of trying to match the subject's gaze, the viewer is privileged to witness the vulnerable act of sleeping. The interaction between the subject of the photograph and the viewer is no longer one of equals; the viewer becomes the voyeur. Yet Spence's subjects are not really sleeping, and therefore interpretations of exhibitionism and soft porn arise.[26] Given the angle of the images, Spence is necessarily poised right over them. The resulting effect is that the viewer is allowed to hover over these figures, not quite dominating them but certainly communing with them in some sort of fashion—on the verge of an erotic encounter, maybe even in a dream-like state.

In 1992 Spence produced a very small series of six self-portraits titled *Dream Sequence*. Interestingly, Spence does not explore self-portraiture overtly in her work, and to follow the argument of this essay and exhibition, all of her pictures are in fact pictures of her. However, there are a few instances when she intentionally photographs herself, and *Dream Sequence* is probably the most prominent example. By pairing the nude female body, seen in an illusive ghostly state against moody night-time images of vacant streets in Montreal, Quebec, and Kiev, Spence creates a quiet and elegant visual metaphor for the state of dreaming in the landscape of both individual and social environments.

Spence possesses exceptional skill in creating images. She does not use photography as a means to an end. It is her dedicated medium and she understands it implicitly, both technically and conceptually. She comes out of the photographic tradition, and through her work she is able to critique the very tradition she represents. Spence's rigorous understanding of the way photography works, with particular regard for the subject/object relationship and the power that is allotted to the viewer, enables her to perform a critical intervention that goes beyond revealing the complex network between photographer, subject, and spectator.[27] Over the course of her 25-year career, Spence has drawn out a collective re-presentation of herself; she has captured aspects of her persona and her psyche without ever having to depict her own physical likeness. Upon viewing the exhibition or reading this catalogue, you may come to think you know and intimately understand Spence as a person, because her portrait shines out and mirrors back at you, through the faces of her friends, family, and community.

NOTES

1
Pernilla Holmes, "In Your Face," *ArtNews* (June 2007): 111. Quote given by American curator Dan Cameron.

2
Roald Nasgaard, "The Portrait and the Facelift," http://www/kwag.on.ca/user_files/images/roald_nasgaard_essay.pdf (2005)

3
David Aurandt, "acknowledgements," *About Face: Portraits and Other Pictures* (Oshawa, Ontario: Robert McLaughlin Gallery, 2005), 1.

4
Ann Thomas, "Witkiewicz, Trčka and Kesting: Pioneers in Modernist Portraiture," *History of Photography* 29, 3 (autumn 2005): 225.

5
Nasgaard.

6
Ibid.

7
Olexander Wlasenko, "about face: portraits and other pictures," *About Face: Portraits and Other Pictures* (Oshawa, Ontario: Robert McLaughlin Gallery, 2005), 8.

8
Abigail Solomon-Godeau, "Photography After Art Photography," *Art After Modernism: Rethinking Representation* (New York: The New Museum of Contemporary Art, 1984), 83.

9
A selection of 11 of these individual portraits by Spence was exhibited in *A Sense of Place: Photography in Manitoba*, The Winnipeg Art Gallery, November 27, 1986 to January 27, 1987. The exhibition was curated by Shirley Madill. In 1987 The Winnipeg Art Gallery purchased *Untitled [Portrait of a Male]* (1986), *Nora Smoking* (1986), and *Jenny* (1986), while *Gerry* (1985) was donated to the permanent collection. These four works were all part of the above-mentioned exhibition.

10
Harold Rosenberg, "Introduction to Avedon's 'Portraits'," *Photography in Print*, Vicki Goldberg, ed. (New York: Simon and Schuster, 1981), 475.

11
Nasgaard.

12
Op cit.

13
Geraldine Wilson worked at The Winnipeg Art Gallery with Sheila Spence in the 1980s. She was responsible for fundraising and was well respected and much liked by her colleagues.

14
Robert Graham, "Here's Me," *Thirteen Essays on Photography* (Canadian Museum of Contemporary Photography, 1988), 2.

15
Donald Kuspit, "Reification or Personalization: The Dilemma of Photography," *C magazine 21* (March 1989): 61.

16
Thomas, 225.

17
Nasgaard.

18
Solomon-Godeau, 80.

19
Holmes, 106.

20
Graham, 6.

21
Author's conversations with artist, 2005-2008.

22
Ibid.

23
Many of the youth in West Broadway were of aboriginal descent. The issue of a white photographer taking images of aboriginal youth was very contentious.

24
André Picard, "On home turf in West Broadway," *Globe and Mail*, January 16, 1999, D2.

25
For a complete overview of this controversy and resulting exhibition, please see Amy Karlinsky, "Sheila Spence on Broadway," *Black/flash* 17, 3 (May 2000): 14–21.

26
Thanks to Denis Longchamps and Frances Thomas for these insights.

27
Solomon-Godeau, 83.

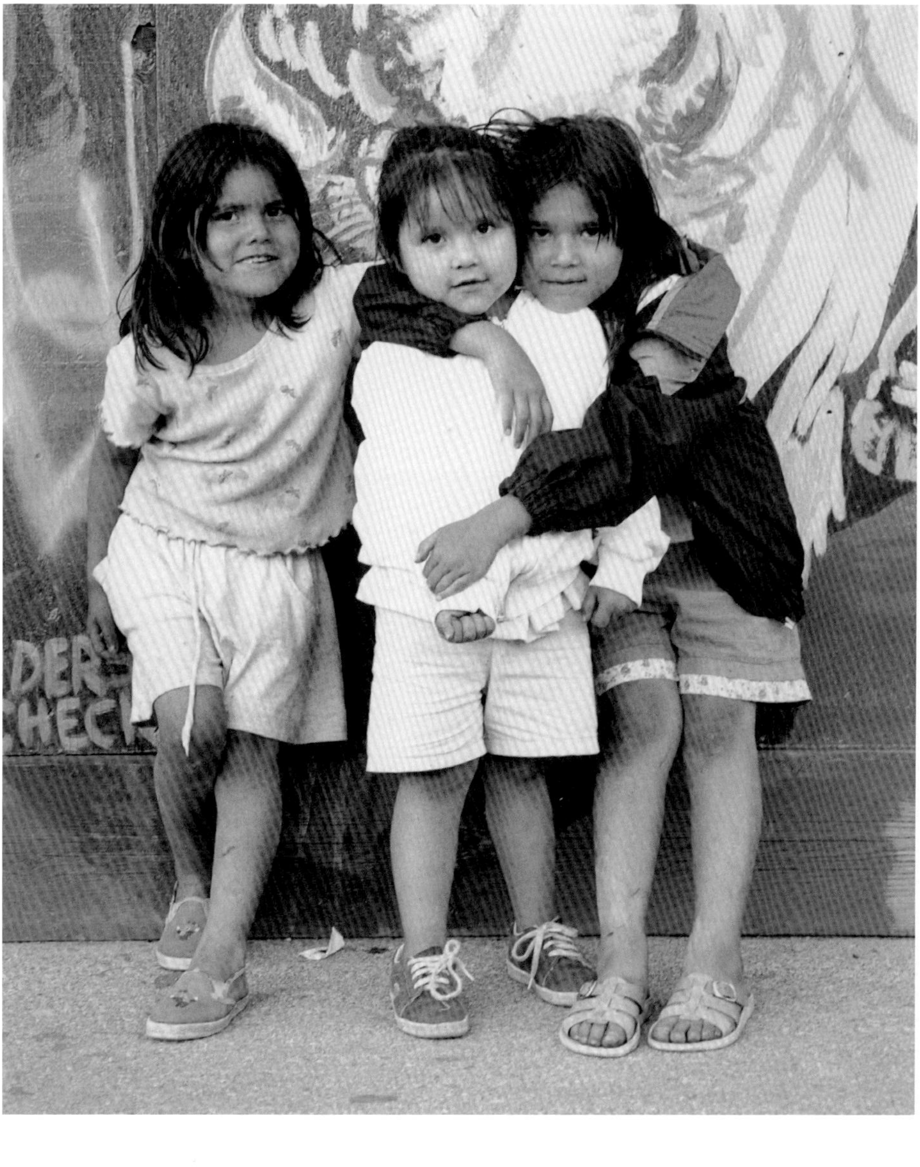

53. *Rachel, Tara, and Angel, West Broadway*, 1998

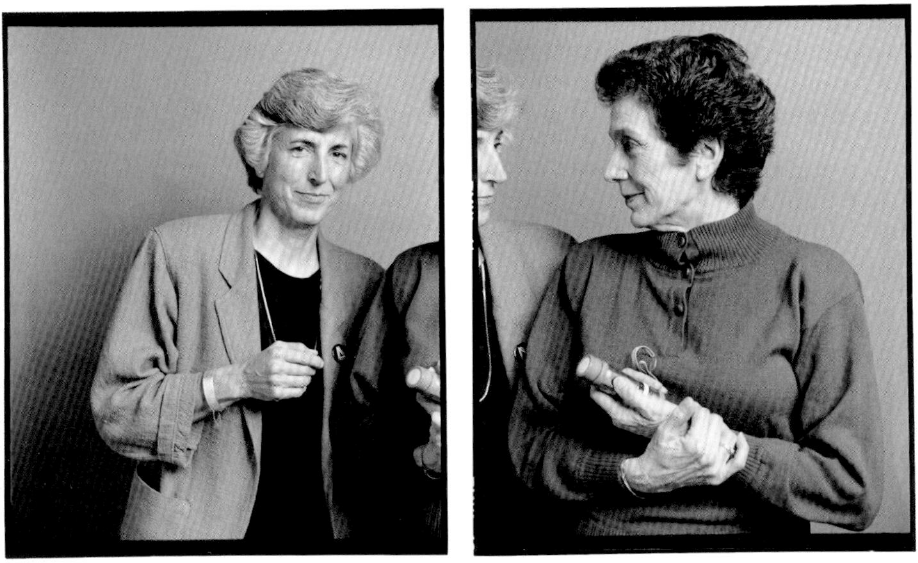

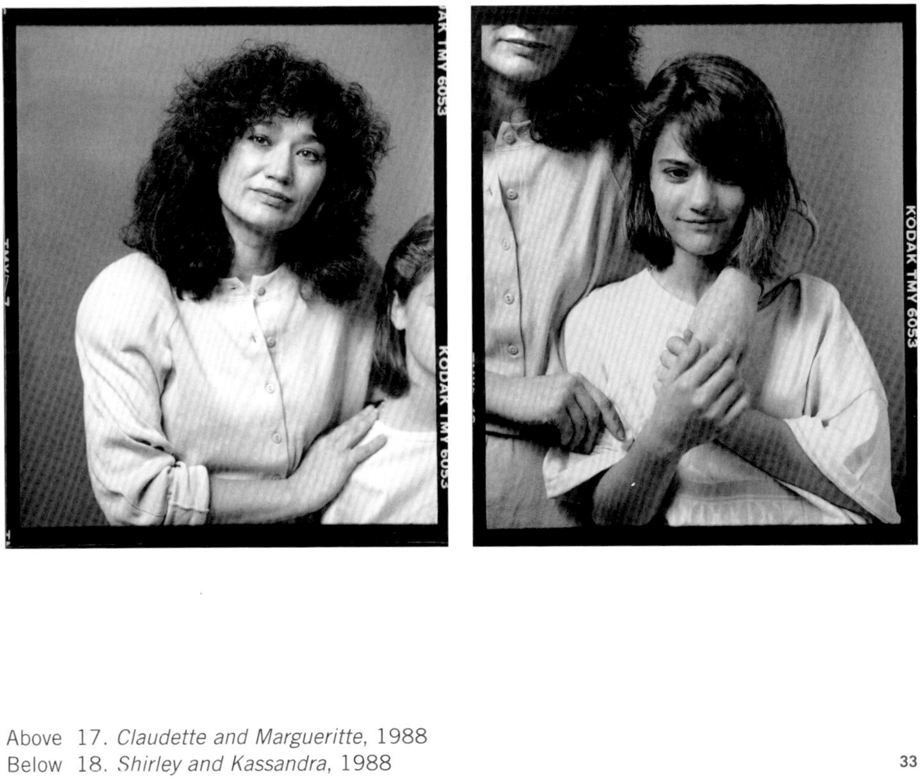

Above 17. *Claudette and Margueritte*, 1988
Below 18. *Shirley and Kassandra*, 1988

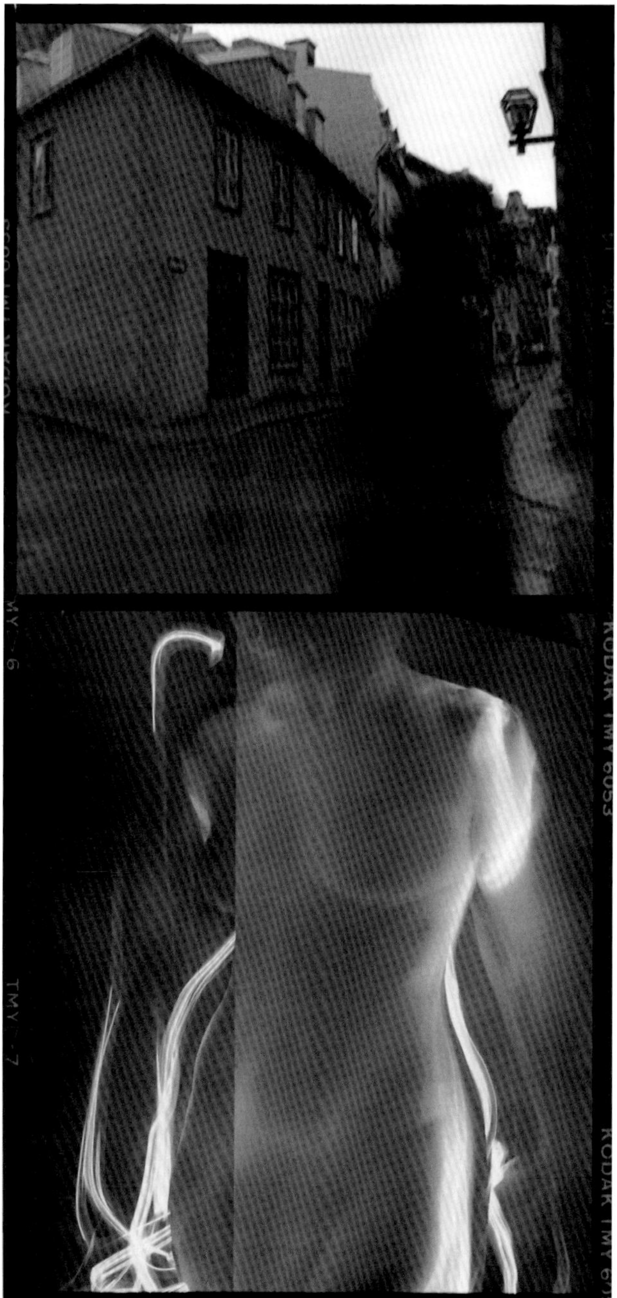

35. *Dream Sequence* [1 of 6], 1992

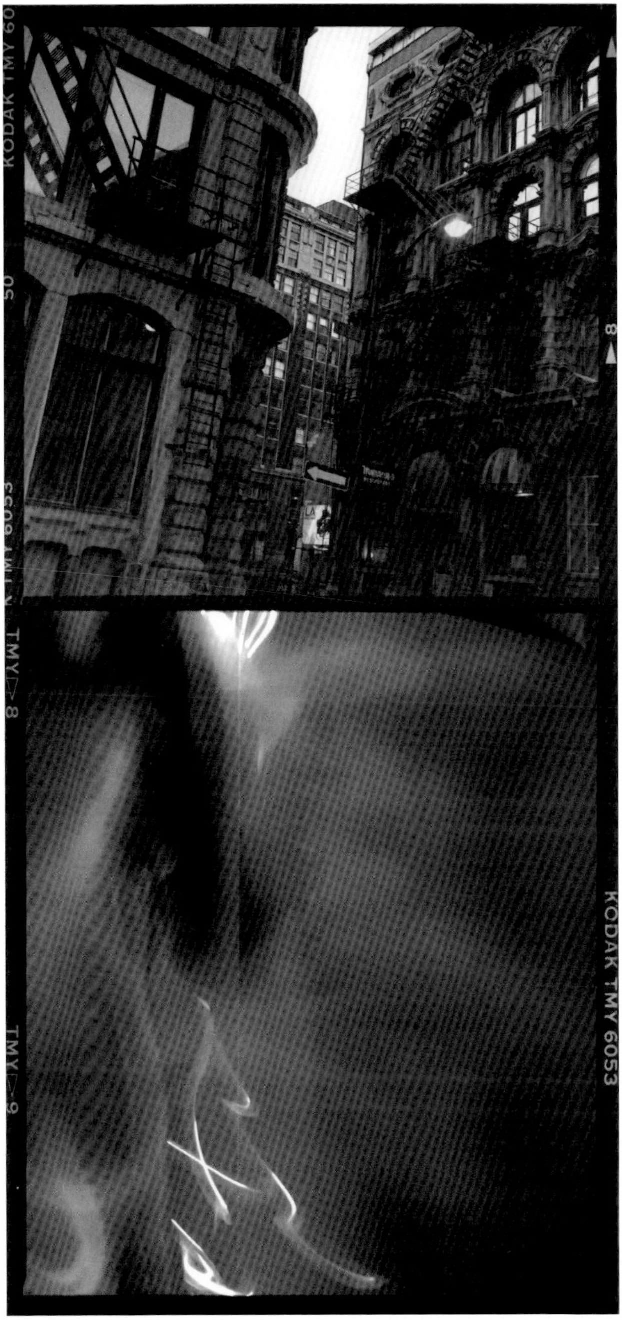

36. *Dream Sequence* [2 of 6], 1992

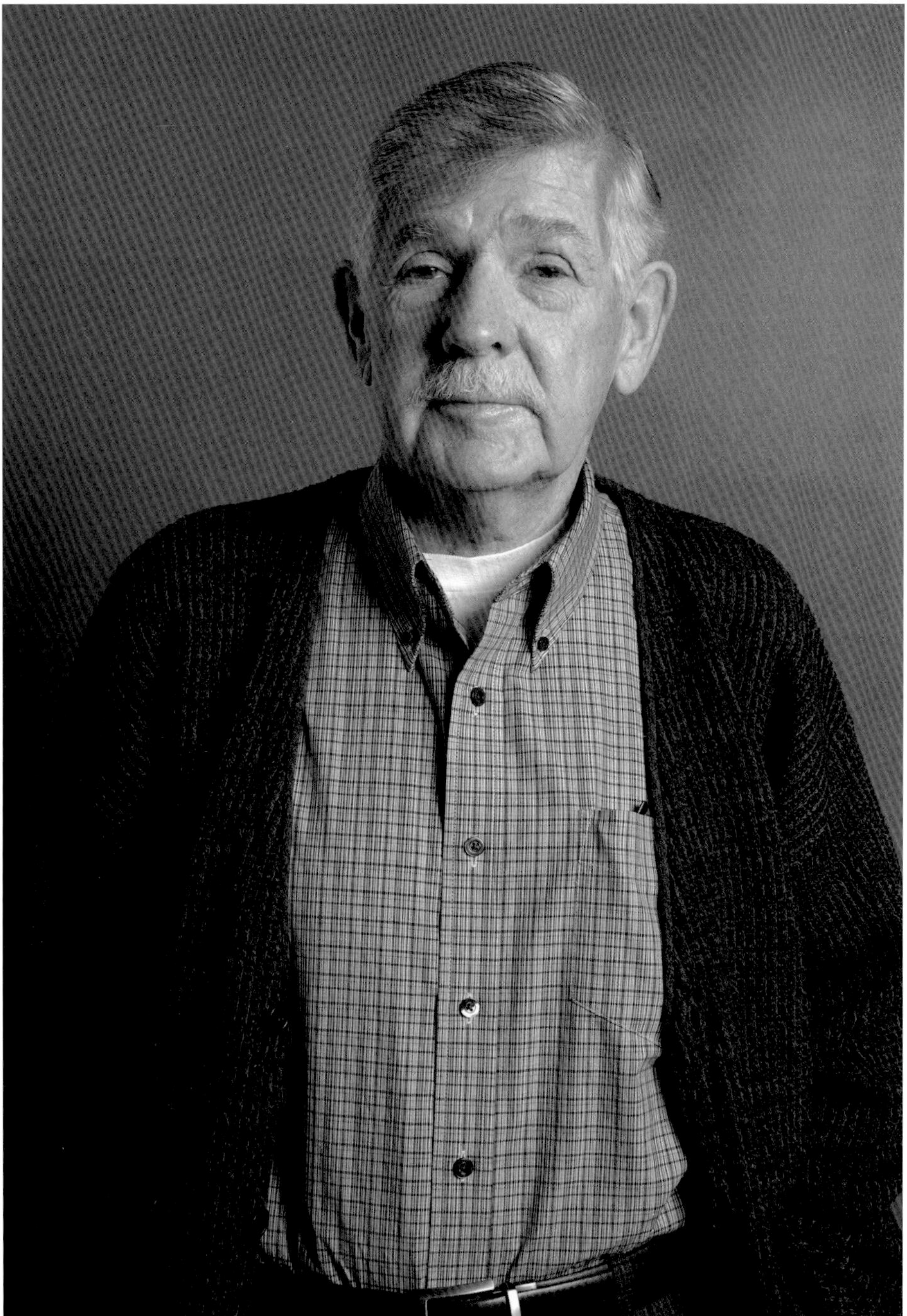

64. *Bill [Dad]*, 2008

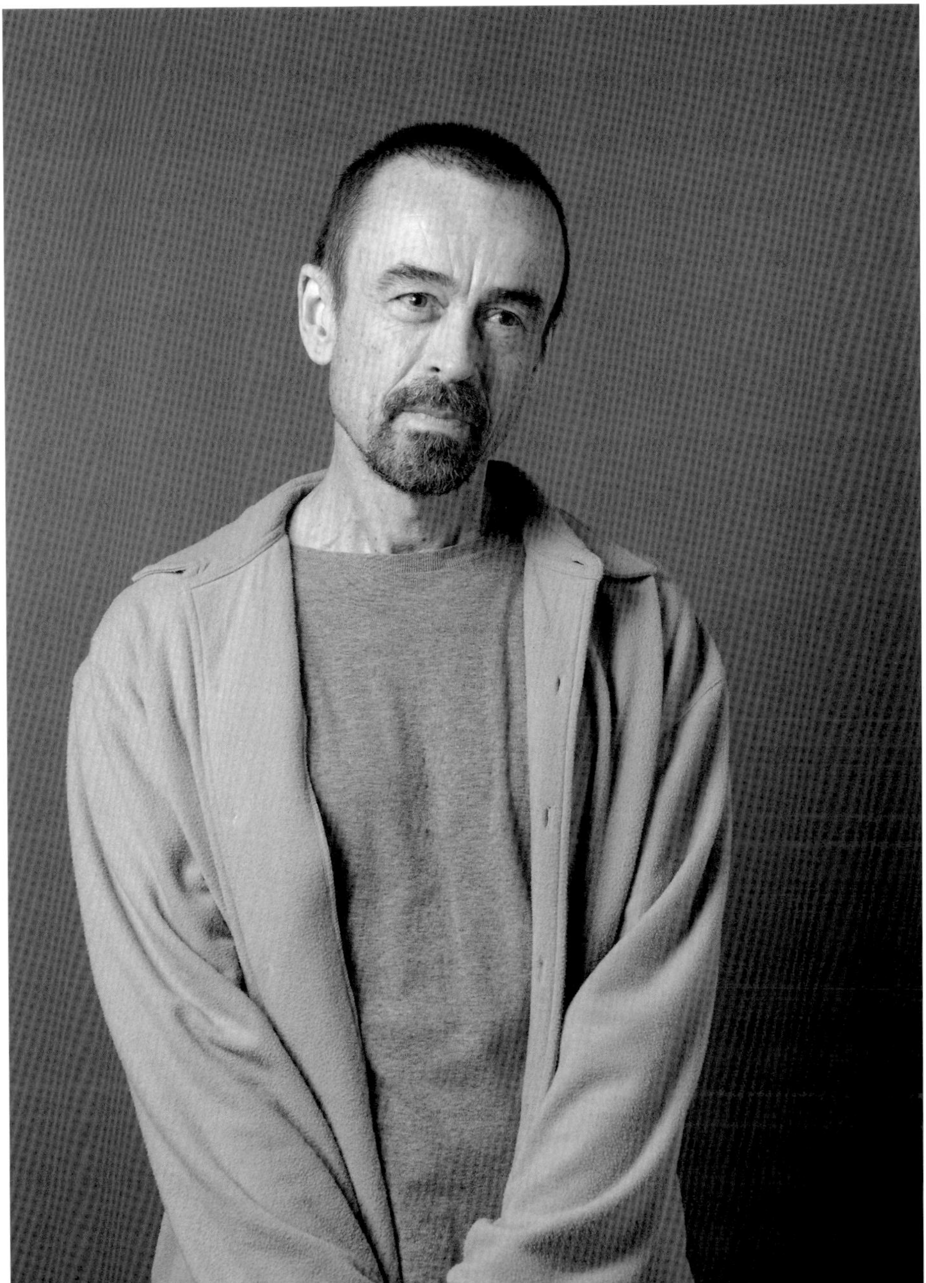

69. *Graham*, 2008

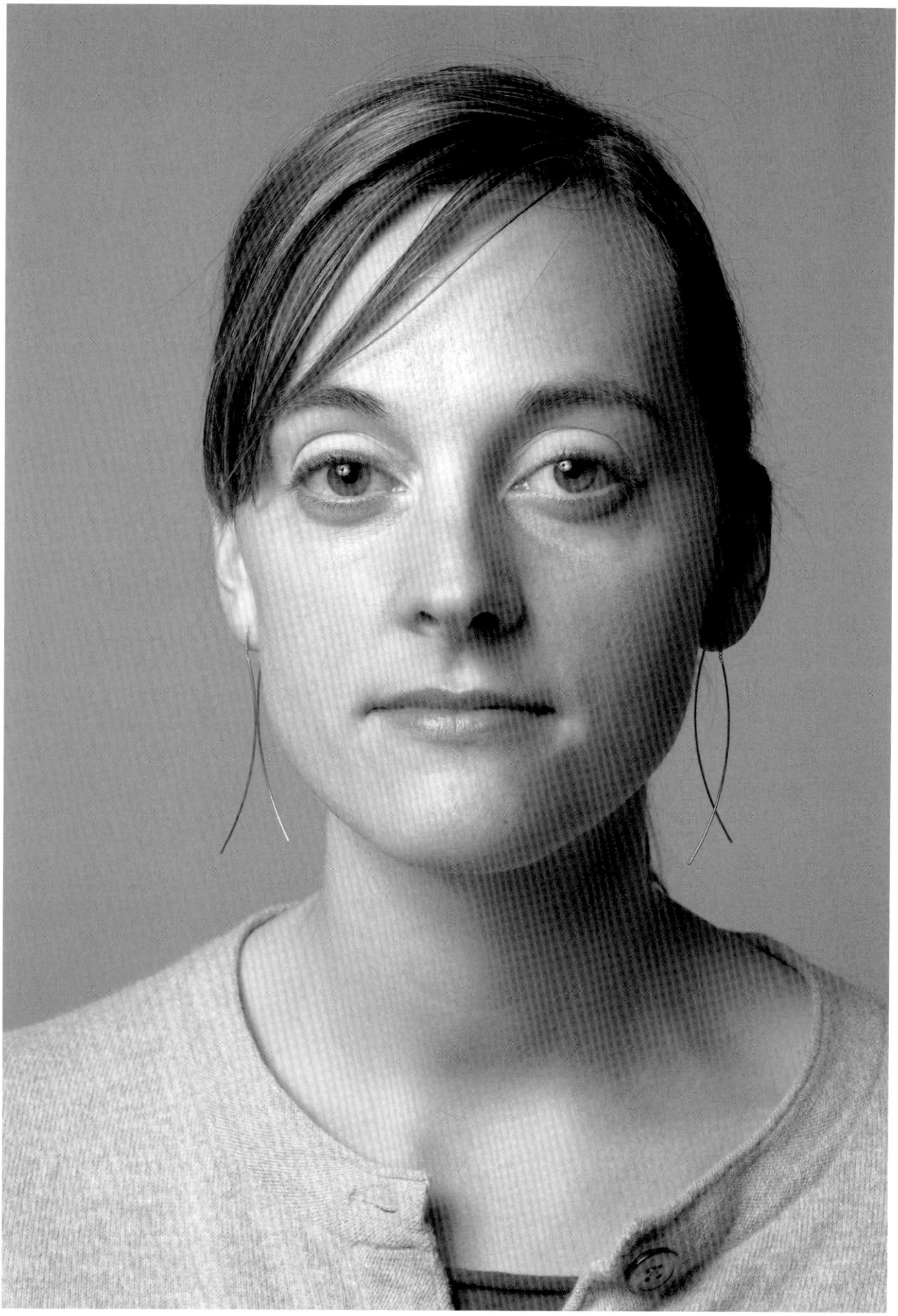

58. *Suzie*, 2007

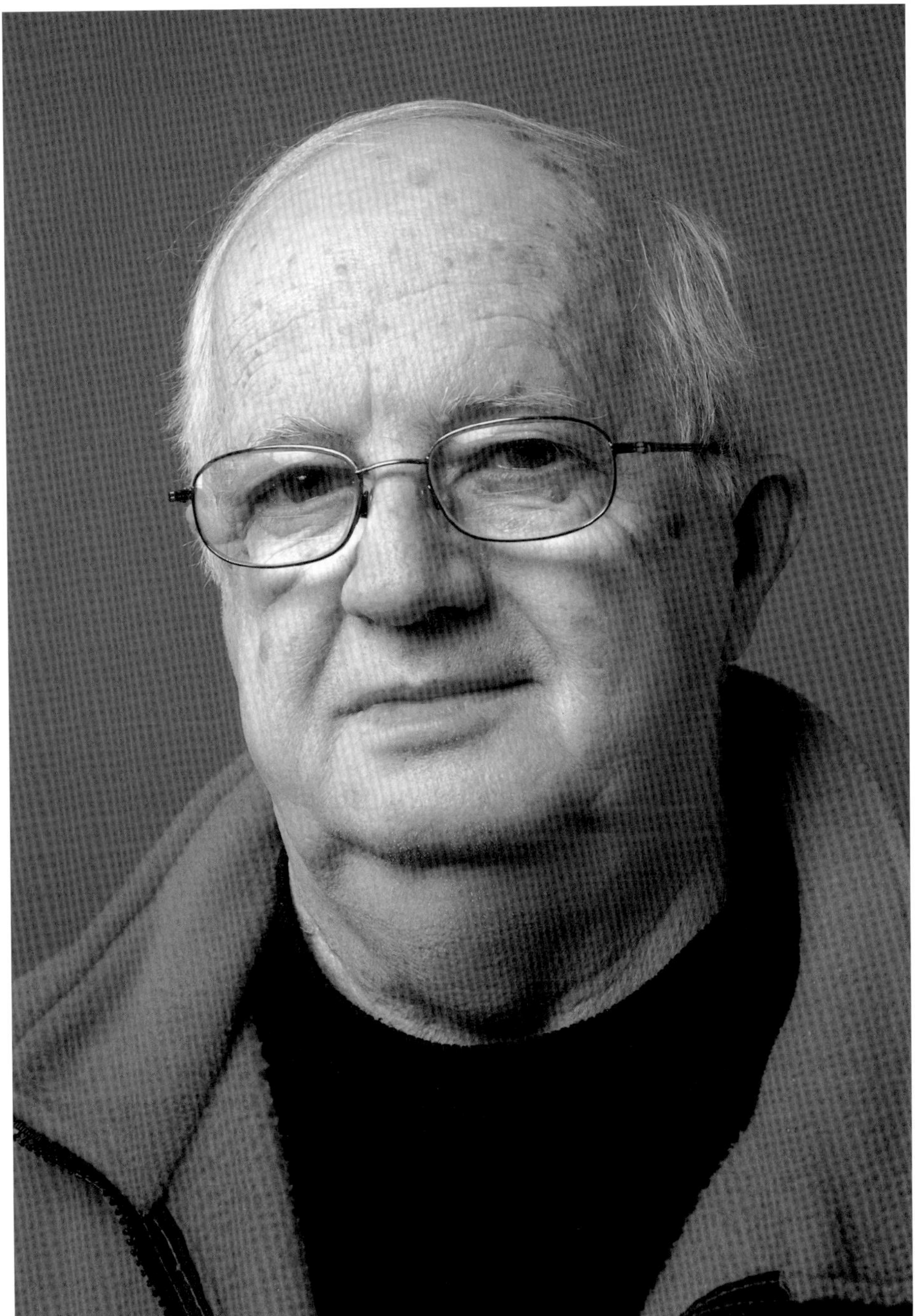

62. *Frank*, 2008

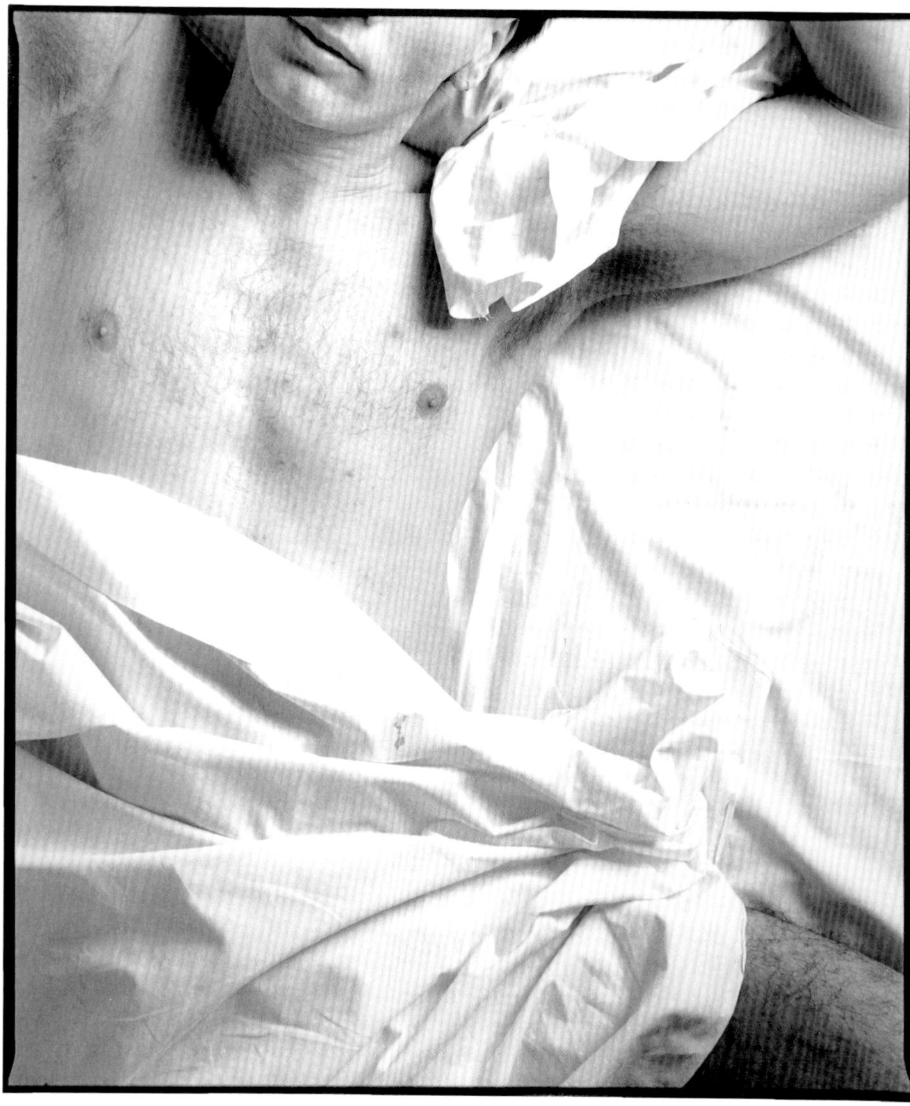

27. *See Whose Face it Wears [#1]*, 1989-90

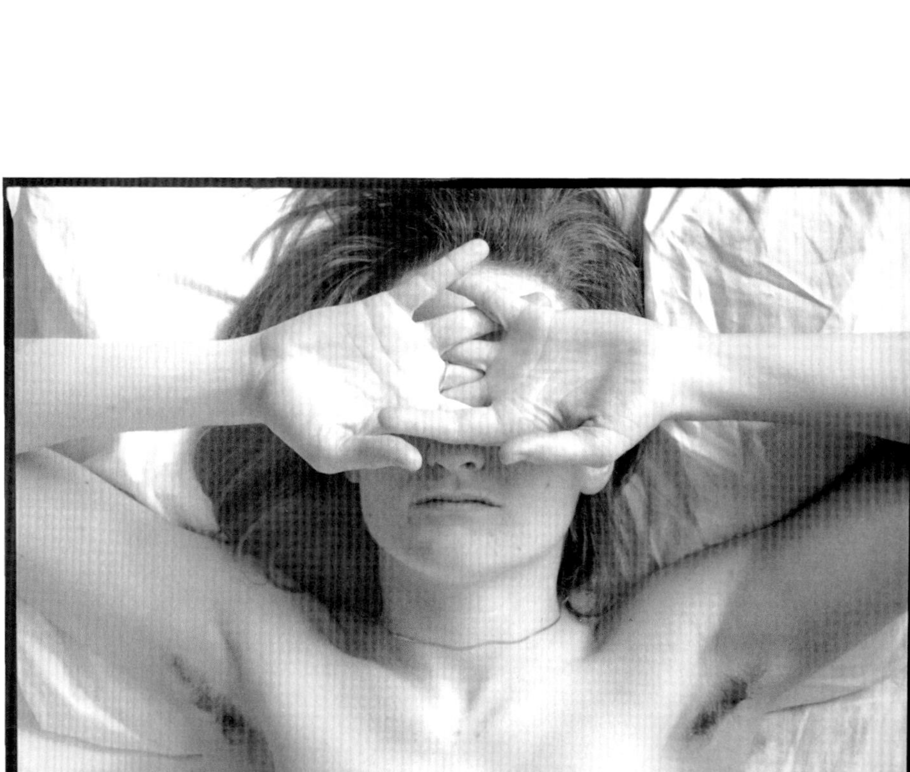

28. *See Whose Face it Wears [#3]*, 1989-90

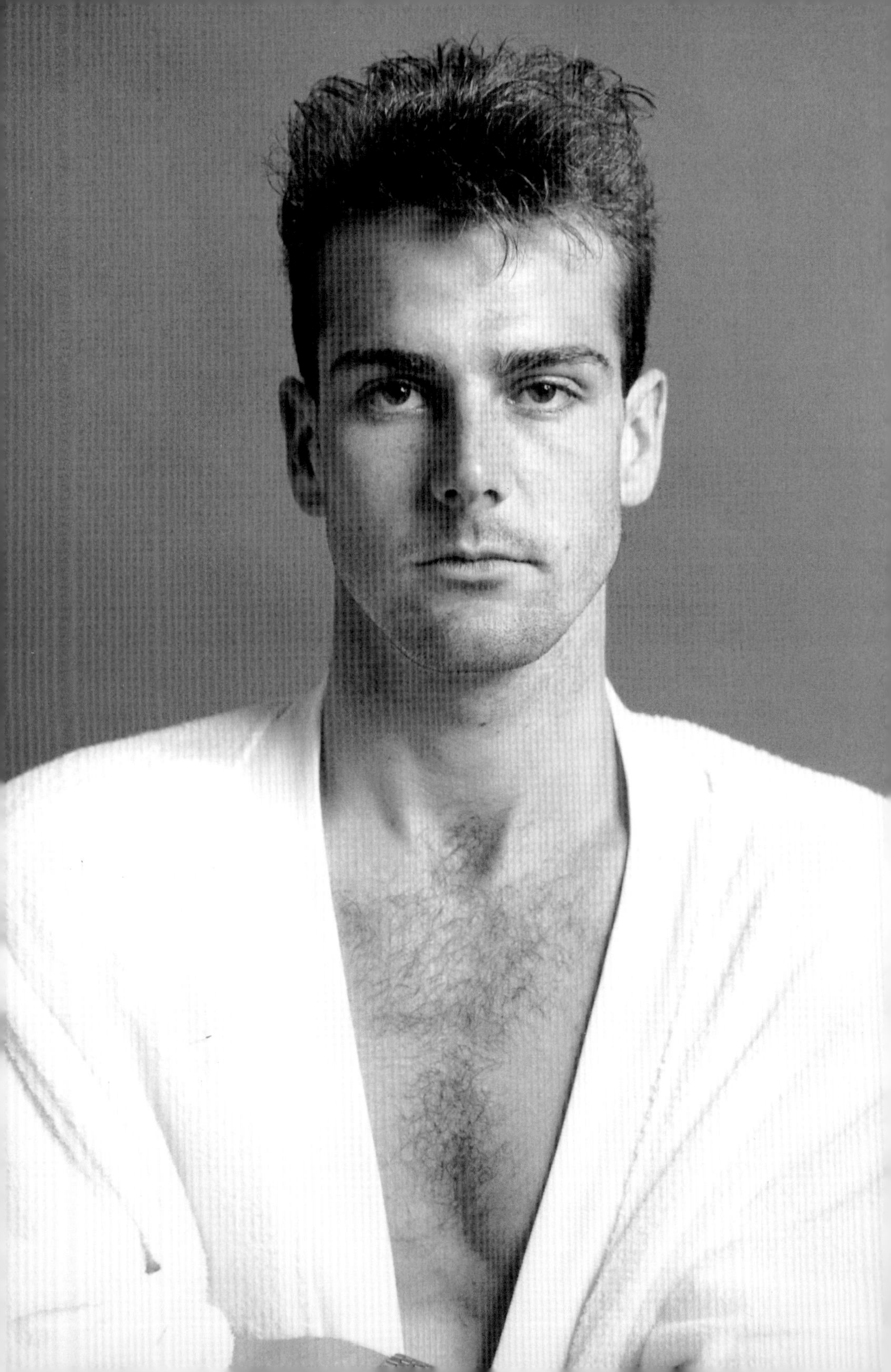

TALK ABOUT PORTRAITS
Robert McKaskell interviews Sheila Spence

I first met Sheila Spence at 10:30am, Friday the 31st of August, 1990. I was a new curator at the WAG and she was the staff photographer assigned to take my picture for publicity. I remember that she got me talking and laughing and made me forget that I was posing in front of the camera. My immediate intuition was that we would be friends. Although I moved from Winnipeg in 1996, we have remained friends for 18 years.

When Sheila asked if I would contribute something to the catalogue of her forthcoming exhibition at the WAG, I told her that I had no background in photography and that I was taking a break from writing, but also that I'd love to have the opportunity to see her and work with her. I had recently done an interview with an artist by e-mail and enjoyed the process. Unlike a "live" interview, each of us had time to give thought to our "conversation" and to edit our responses. We decided to give it a try. To prepare for the interview we spent three afternoons together earlier this month looking at, and talking about, the work. What follows occurred a few weeks later.

RM Your exhibition includes portraits taken over a span of 25 years. There are three types: portraits of individual friends, group portraits in which each

11. *Billy*, 1986

member of the group is featured in a separate frame, and photographs of children and youths from your former neighbourhood in the West Broadway district of Winnipeg.

Let's start with the individuals. You subvert our expectations of a portrait by placing your subjects in front of a neutral background and identifying them (with a few exceptions) only by their first names. Since they aren't placed in a social context and there is no visual information to allow the development of a narrative, we are left even more alone with the subject than is usual with a photograph. This is analogous to being in front of an abstract painting, if perhaps a little less intimidating. Most of us have more experience with photography than painting—both because we have probably taken pictures and because photography is the ubiquitous medium of the twentieth century. How would you have us start looking at these portraits?

SS I think when the subject is looking into the camera lens, in fact making eye contact with the viewer, the viewer first looks at the eyes. It's a little like having a conversation with the person in the photograph. In conversation we make eye contact. Because this conversation is one-sided, the viewer then has licence to study other details in the image. The viewer's eye wanders. There are a few portraits where the subject does not make eye contact. In this case I respond to the portrait as I would to a shy person. For an instant I find myself averting my eyes.

RM Aha! I'm looking at a reproduction of *Billy* (1986) in a magazine. It's true. His eyes draw me in, and then my eyes move around his face. You've lit the photograph from the right, so I notice his left eyebrow. The hairs grow along the top of his brow except near the nose, where they curve in a different direction, like a cowlick. And his hair curls down toward the eyebrow. He's a hairy guy. There's stubble on his face; he probably has to shave twice a day to avoid a five o'clock shadow. I go on to the chest hair, the robe, up to the ears, and suddenly I realize that I've been with the image for twenty minutes.

The magazine is *Border Crossings* (Winter, 1986). In his introduction to your photographs, Robert Enright says, "Out of the lean visual information we're given, we invent the personalities of the subjects." Concerning Billy he writes, "[he] simply looks bored. He has a spade chin and a wide enough expanse of terry-toweled shoulder to act as a stand-in for a football player from Dukes of Hazard University." Comparing Billy's portrait to another, he notes Billy's "studied indifference." None of these things would have occurred to me. Although the subject is a particular person, I generalize about the image. I see a good-looking young man who seems comfortable with himself. What was your procedure for these photographs? How did you instruct your subjects?

SS In Billy's 1986 portrait I don't see indifference, although I think that may have been what he was going for. In Billy's portrait I see an underlying uncertainty with a semi-transparent overlay of rock star. His projected persona is not entirely convincing. But again, like Robert, I am using these portraits of others as a vehicle for my own thoughts.

When I took these photographs I used a fairly narrow neutral grey seamless paper as a backdrop. I asked the subjects to stand in front of and away from the backdrop and limit their movements within the narrow field. My camera was on a tripod because the lighting required a slow shutter speed and this allowed me to engage in conversation while I was taking the photographs. During these sessions each person would change position, sometimes only slightly, while we talked, and I would take a number of photographs.

RM You, Robert, and I all use the portraits as vehicles of our own thoughts. The difference is that yours are more acute because you know the people and shot the film. While I understand both your and Robert's readings and they might influence my thoughts, my responses remain my own. The portrait leaves room for each of us to have a different interpretation—and those interpretations mirror our individual sensibilities.

What considerations led to the photograph you kept of each person?

SS This is where my answers become less certain, Bob. When I am reviewing the photos that I have taken of each person, I go through all of them. Sometimes there is one that just jumps out at me. That becomes my choice. More often on the first review I discard all of the images that don't work, leaving fewer than a handful to consider. I enlarge the remaining images and again, look at them closely. From these I may find one image that I respond to at an emotional level, sometimes not.

When I began the recent work for this exhibition, I took many photographs of various people before I had something that worked for me. Calvin and Andrew were my break-through images. I photographed Calvin late in 2006 and Andrew several months later. Between these two I also took other portraits, none of them successful. By the time I photographed Andrew, I was beginning to lose faith in the process and my abilities to make the images that I had planned to make.

RM Did you follow the same procedure for the recent portraits? How did using a digital camera change things?

SS In the recent portraits, I used much the same process as in the old work. Instead of a seamless paper backdrop, I used a wall painted a mid-range tone. I mindfully chose to take these photos the same way they were taken twenty years ago. By reducing the variables in the photo sessions I hoped to hone in on what has changed in either the subject's or my point of view over time. This work is photographed digitally and in colour. It is dropped back to black and white in the computer before printing. There are technical differences using digital technology; a different skill set is needed to prepare the captured file for print, for example. Capturing the image is much the same as shooting with film. Lighting, focus, composition, exposure, are essentially the same skills.

RM I wonder if it's possible for a viewer to discern a point of view. I'm looking at a print of a JPEG of *Billy* (2008). The hair-growth pattern along the eyebrow is the same, but the hair has been trimmed (or plucked—I don't have enough definition on this print to tell). He's clean-shaven. I get the idea that he's taken care of himself, because his complexion is good, his eyes are as bright as they were twenty-two years ago, and the lines on his face appear there simply because of aging—the force of physical, rather than mental, gravity. There are no lines that suggest years of frowning, nor are there lines that suggest years of laughing. In this portrait you include two fingers of his left hand, and there's the shock. The nails are cut to the quick! Are they bitten? Worn? Unlike the earlier portrait, I find it difficult to reduce this portrait to a generalization. It has more detail, but I wonder to what degree that is related to the technology. The subject is more specific, but is that because he has accumulated a few more decades of life's experiences? What is a point of view?

One thing I've been thinking about while looking at these images is how much I am missing the quality and size of your prints. It's a little like looking at pictures of paintings in a book. To what degree do you think of your photographs as objects?

SS In my new portraits, I believe I am more aware of my point of view in my choice of image. For example, I had two or three images of Billy that were quite similar in expression and in posture that I was considering. I chose the image that showed his fingernails. As subtle a detail as that is, I felt it was enough information to possibly subvert a predictable narrative.

I do think of my photographs as objects. I preferred the old fibre-based silver paper to the new matte-surfaced rag paper of the digital printer. The

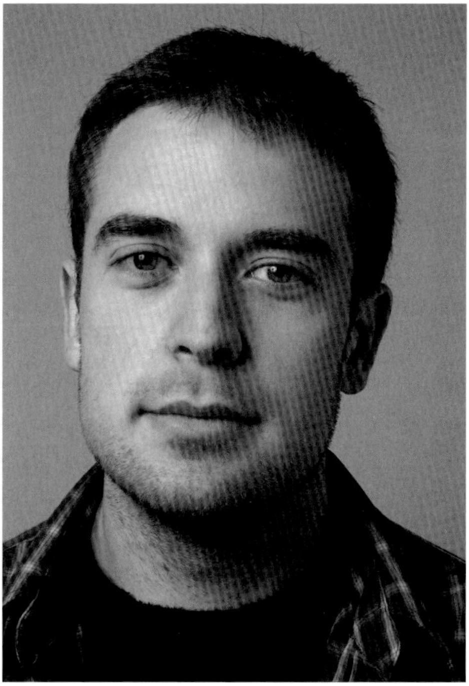

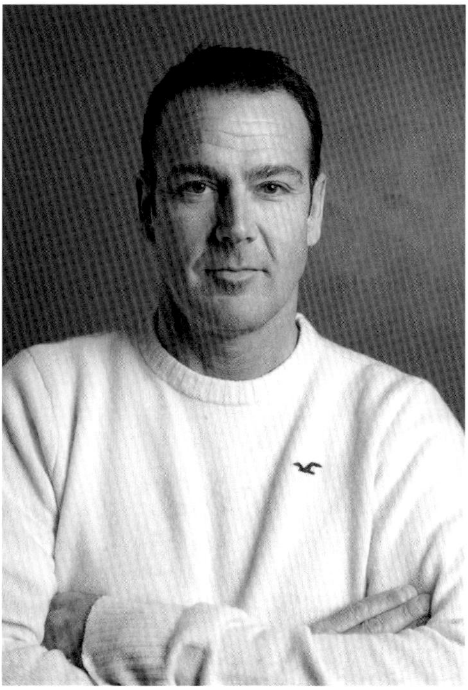

Above 59. *Andrew*, 2007
Below 67. *Billy*, 2008

digital printer is capable of outputting an image that comes quite close to the glossy prints on fibre-based paper, but the weight and feel of it is quite different. Because photographic technology has changed, I don't see any point in trying to make the new prints appear to be silver prints, but I do miss them.

RM The digital prints have a larger range of tonality and clearer definition of detail that make them sumptuous.

Your "portraits in series" suggest narratives, not least because the interactions among the individuals in the various groups are so different. How did you go about making these works?

SS After the individual portraits, I was interested in showing individuals within their chosen family. At the same time I didn't want to lose the sense of the individual to a group portrait, so again I asked friends and family (people with whom I was close) to allow me to photograph them and to choose those with whom they would like to be photographed. Many chose family for their portraits—sons, daughters, and partners—and a few chose long-time friends (*Nancy, Robin, Alison, and Jamie*).

When taking these photographs, I asked the subjects to place themselves as they would in a traditional group shot, lined up in front of the camera. Then I took a number of photographs of each individual in the group, moving the camera for each one. Afterwards I selected an image of each person and assembled them into a grouping. What I found particularly interesting in this process was the interaction of the people on the edges of the frame. When an individual was being photographed, each interacted with me, but those who thought they were off-camera interacted with each other. This action at the edges of the frame, as minimal as it was, contextualized the group dynamic. Often what was happening at the edge implied a much richer narrative.

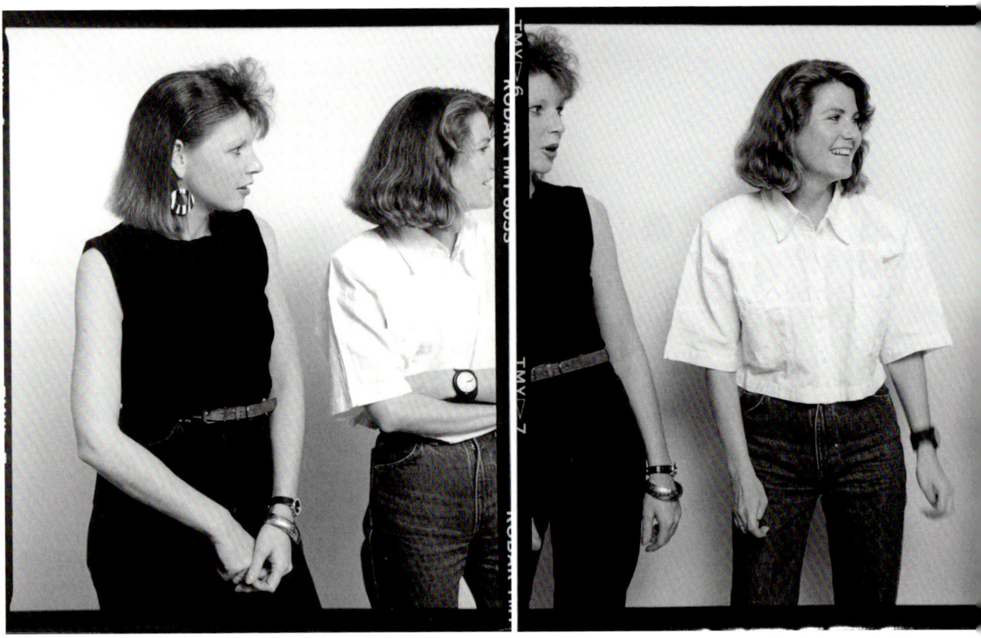

RM Now I understand how you got those great profiles of Sharon in *Sharon and Bob* (1989) and *Kim and Sharon* (2007). This body of work concentrates on the dynamics of relationships. You present, very subtly, emotions that range from barely suppressed tension to sheer joy.

The work we've talked about so far is very personal both because the subjects are your friends and family and because viewers reveal themselves in their responses to it. On the other hand, *The Images of West Broadway* are public. These are the kids we pass on the street (although we may not take the time to look at them) and they are photographed in urban settings. Although you began the project for personal reasons—to better understand the youths in your neighbourhood—it generated public debate. This echoes the response to the billboard projects concerning homophobia you did with Noreen Stevens (as the artist collective Average Good Looks) in the early 1990s. Do you see the role of photography as being different in these works?

22. *Nancy, Robin, Alison, and Jamie*, 1989

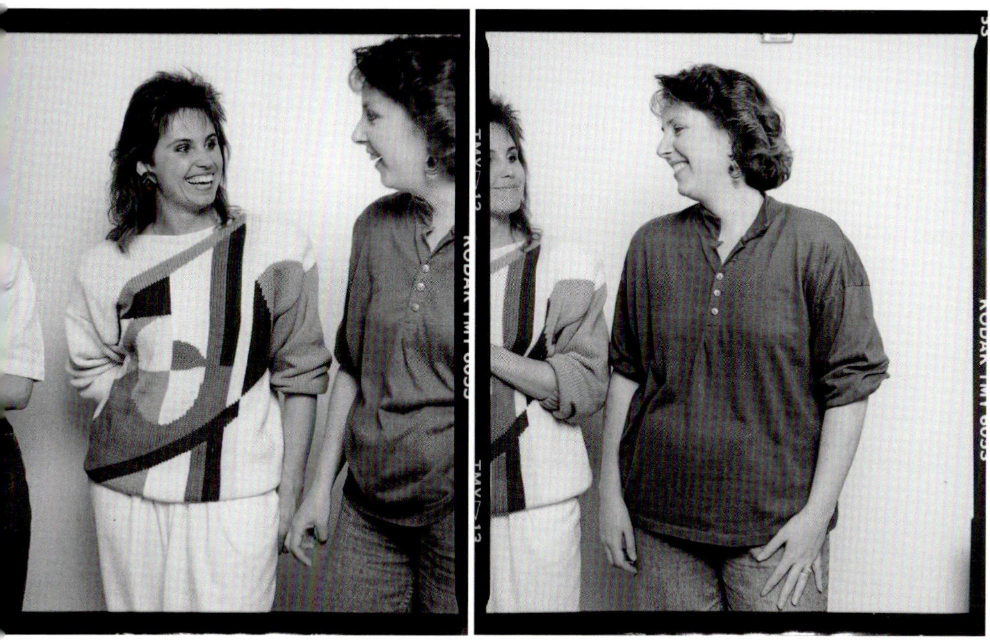

SS Yes and no. That is to say that I think all of my work is informed by my personal politics; in fact, I think that the way one lives or moves through the world is a political statement. The difference between most of my work and the two projects that you have identified is that both the Average Good Looks work and my *Images of West Broadway* directly addressed hot-button issues that were making headlines at that time.

The Average Good Looks work began in response to a gay bashing which ended in a death. Many, or at the very least some, people would have witnessed this incident and yet there was no intervention. When I learned of this, I immediately drew a parallel to the Montreal Massacre of fourteen women in 1989 where the killer claimed to be "fighting feminism." If the Montreal Massacre was misogyny carried to the extreme, I felt that the 1991 murder of Gordon Kuhtey in Winnipeg was evidence of homophobia taken to its extreme conclusion. With both anti-feminism and homophobia there were, and to some extent still are, "socially acceptable" levels of

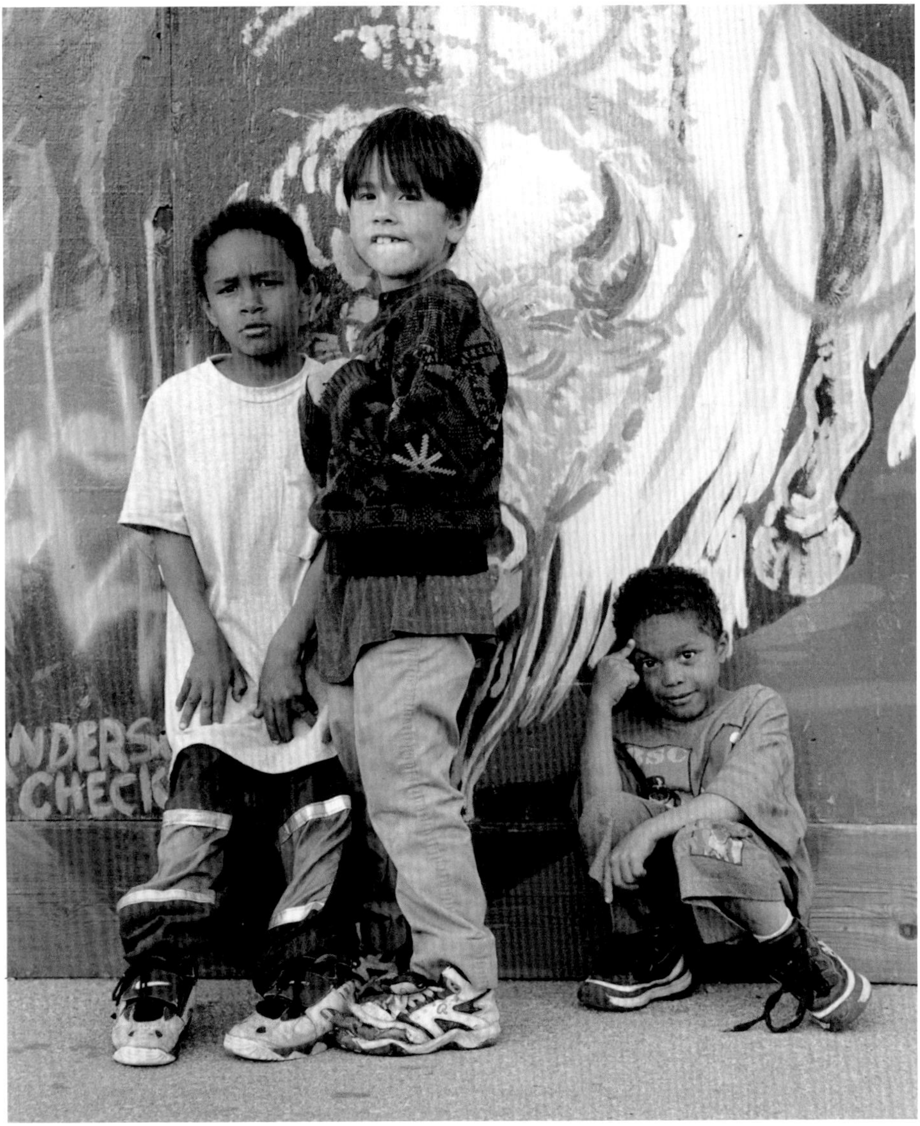

52. *Timothy, Shane, and Tyrone, West Broadway,* 1998

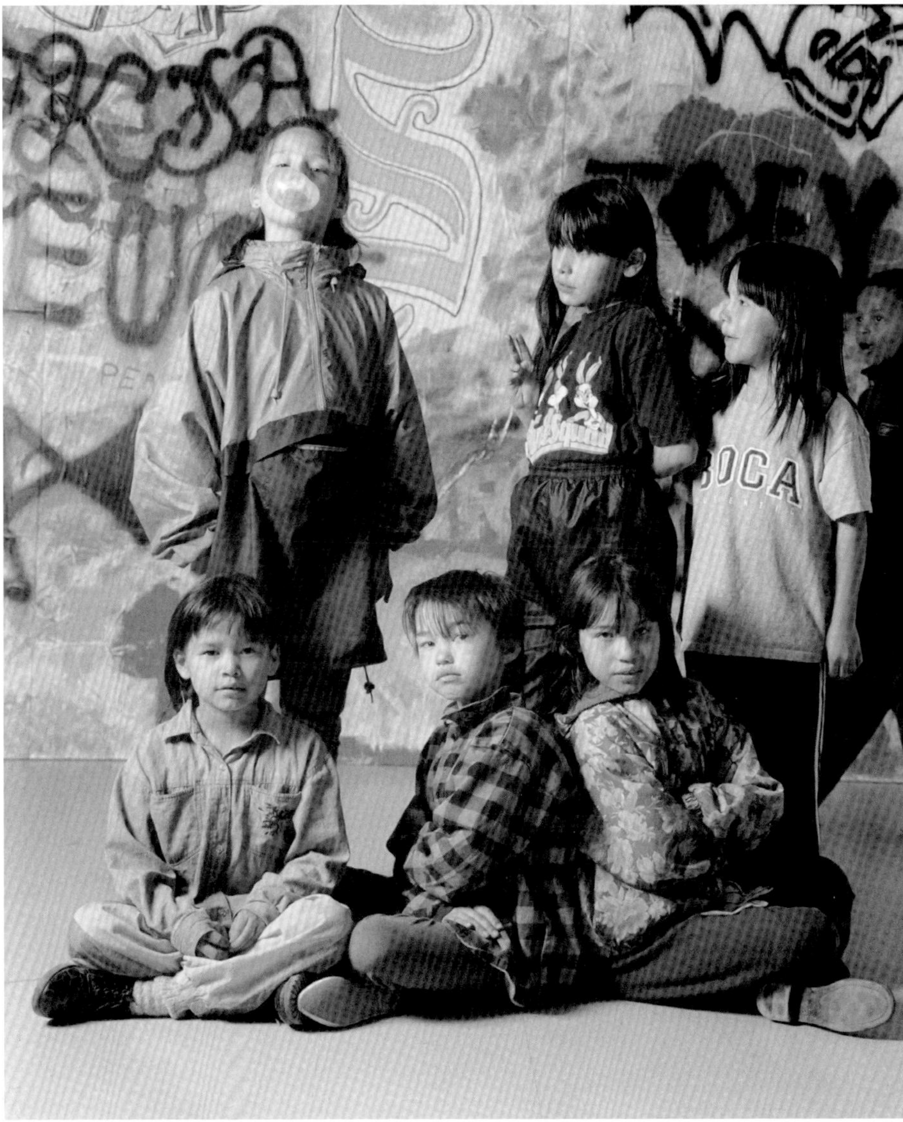

41. *Stacie and Friends, West Broadway,* 1997

expression. Average Good Looks' first work was in response to Mr. Kuhtey's death and the response was public (on a billboard) and timely. I expected a public response to this work.

Again, with *Images of West Broadway* I was, in part, addressing current events. My neighbourhood, West Broadway, was a subject of much media attention, primarily for incidents of youth violence. Prior to beginning this work, West Broadway had made the headlines so often it was identified in the press as "Murder's Half Acre." My house at that time backed onto a park where I could watch groups of youth gathering most evenings, and rather than continue to feel my stress level build with the escalation of the media coverage, I decided to meet the neighbourhood through this photographic project. Over the two-year stretch that I worked on this project, I did get to know some of the teenagers that I photographed. Many of the boys would come to my house, sit on the porch and pour through the contact sheets of the photo sessions. I actually took a group of five of the boys to my studio one afternoon and I did a series of studio shots of them. I have never exhibited those images because the boys felt uncomfortable and out of place in the studio. My relationship to these subjects was fragile due to our differences. I haven't seen any of them since exhibiting the work in 1999.

RM In the West Broadway photographs your subjects pose for you somewhat self-consciously. It's ironic that they revealed more than you knew. It was partly their use of hand gestures that upset some people and led to the controversy surrounding the exhibition. Would you tell me again the analogy Carol Shields drew between writing and photography?

SS Some years ago I was asked to photograph Carol and Donald Shields. Their children wanted a portrait of the two of them together in their academic robes. At the beginning of this shoot Carol said that there were many parallels between the photographic process and the writing process.

Photographers, like writers, begin with an idea of a character and from the initial conception, through the dimly lit process, the character develops. Both rely on the structure of the process to take them to a conclusion and that conclusion is not apparent at the beginning. (This was a long time ago and I am relying on memory here.) With all of my photographs this has been the case, but it is certainly more apparent to me with West Broadway, where I did not know the people I photographed and where my only expectation was that I would learn something about them.

RM While we were talking in Winnipeg a few weeks ago you said, "I start with a notion of what I want, but I have to adjust to what I've got. When you start a shoot it's like being on a ride. You can't just stop to make an adjustment. There's serendipity about doing this work. It feels like life that way." And in another context: "The fibre of relationships you develop over time keeps weaving into what you do."

You have titled this exhibition after a quote from Richard Avedon: "Sometimes I think all my pictures are just pictures of me. My concern is ... the human predicament, only what I consider the human predicament may simply be my own." What I get as a picture of you through this work is a sense of your acute self-awareness and the completely non-judgmental openness you take to people.

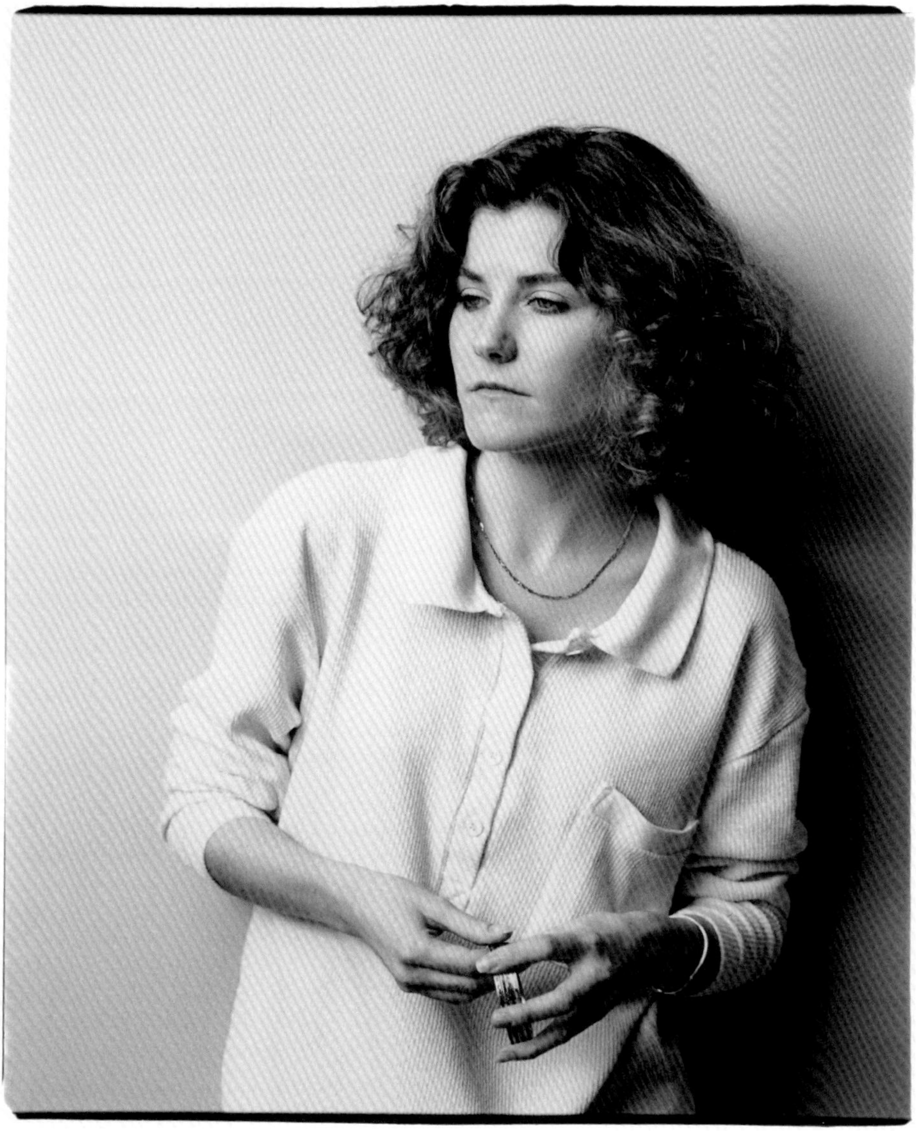

10. *Robin*, 1986

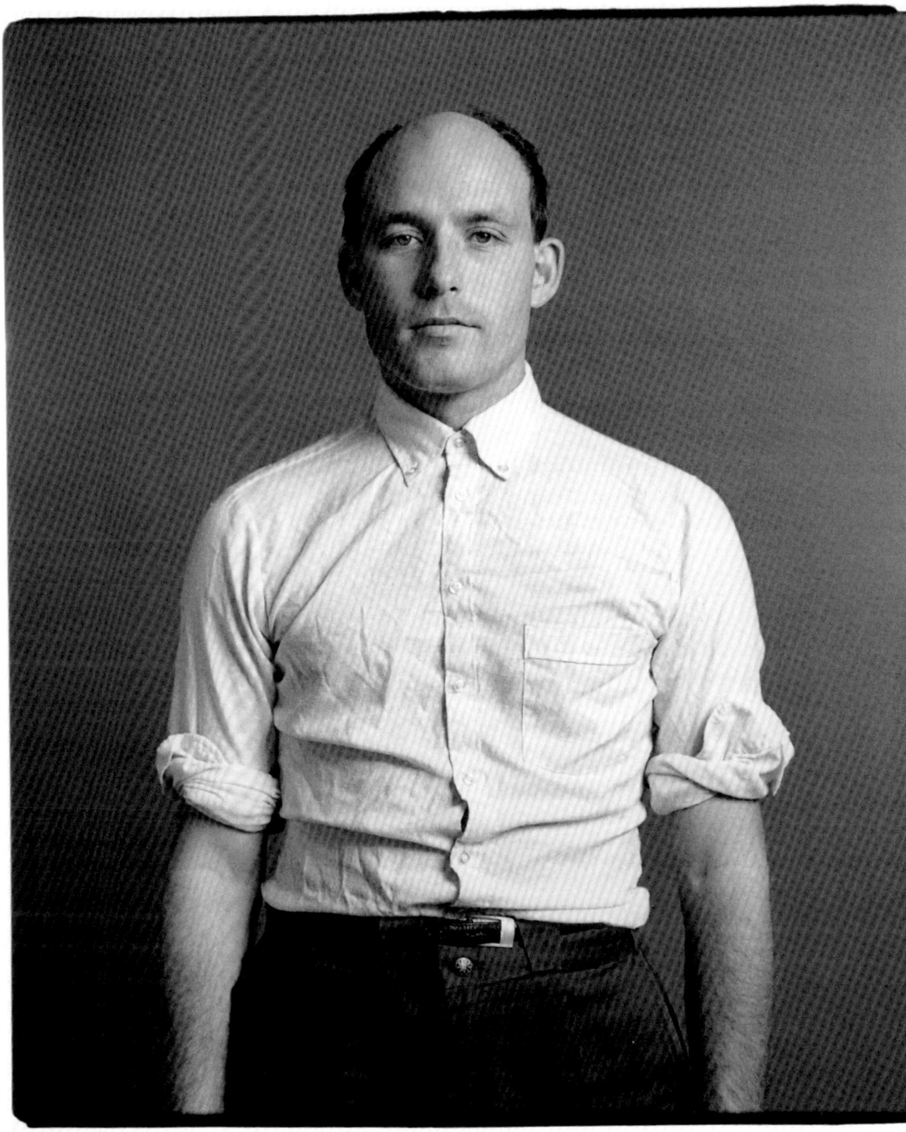

1. *Scott*, 1984

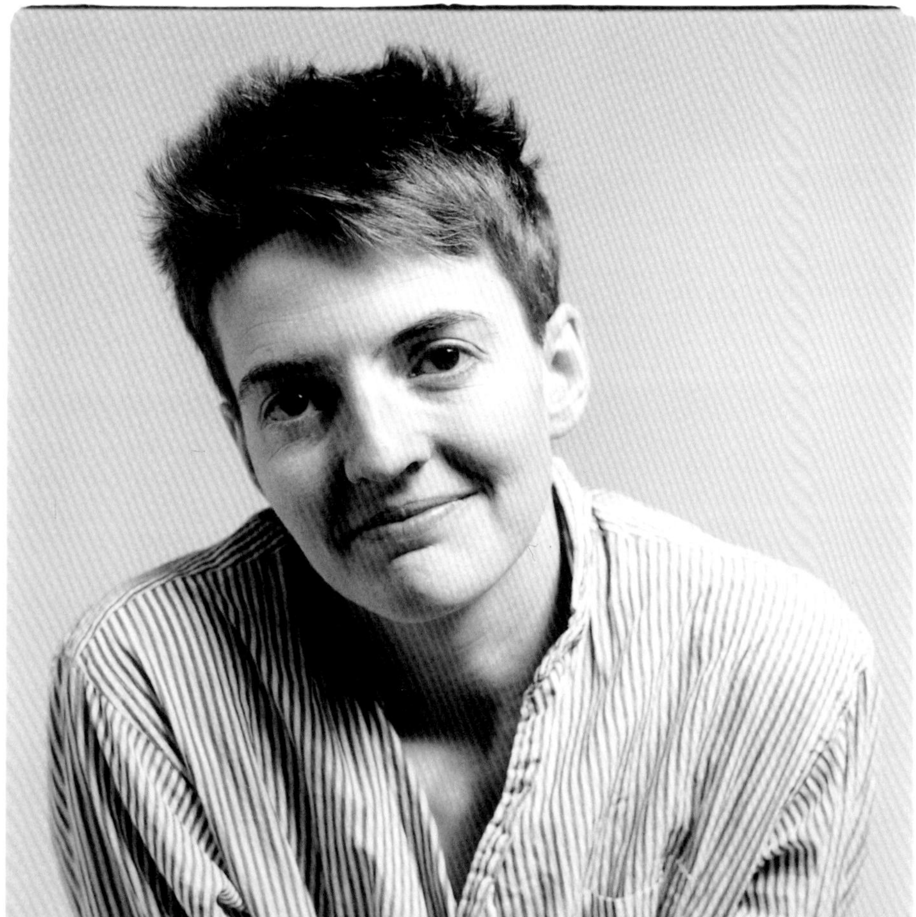

15. *Jude*, 1988

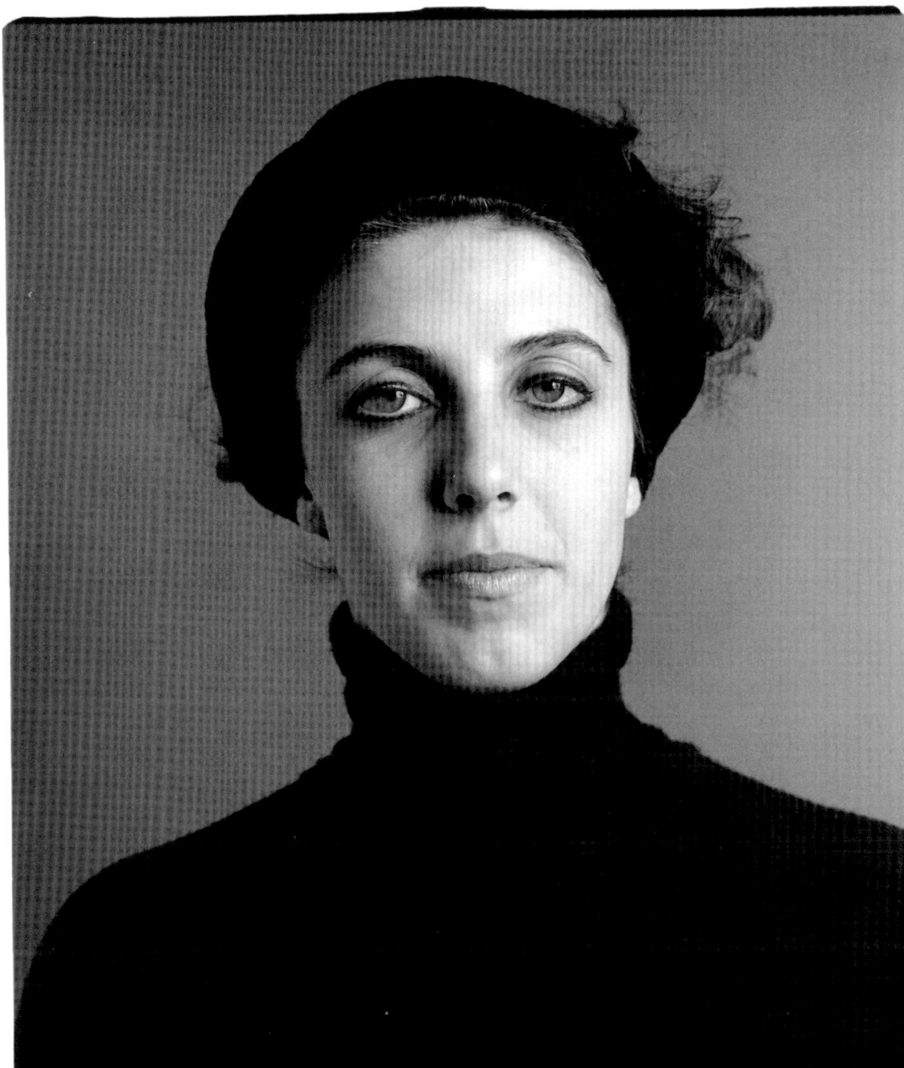

12. *Nora*, 1986

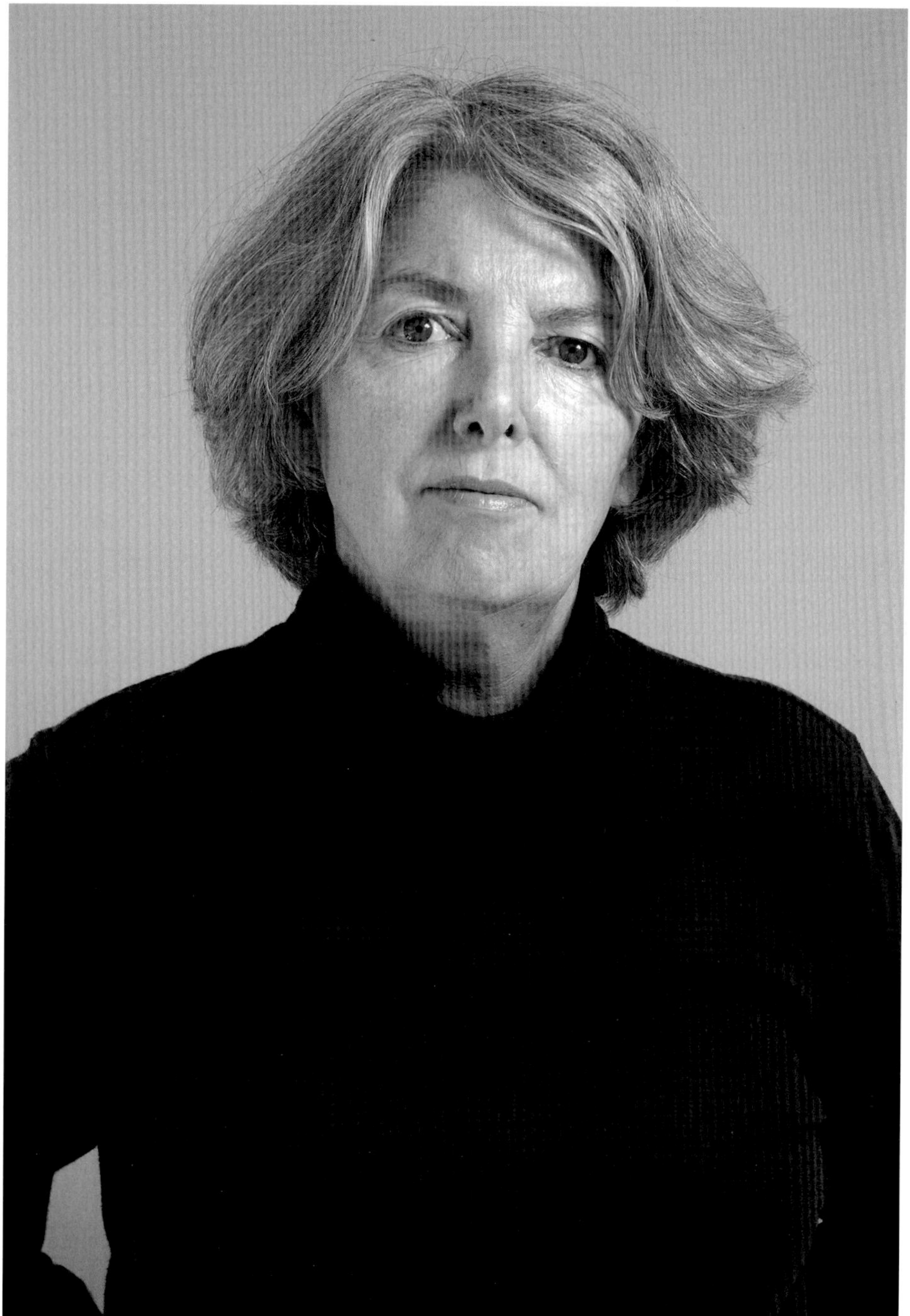

65. *Wendy*, 2008

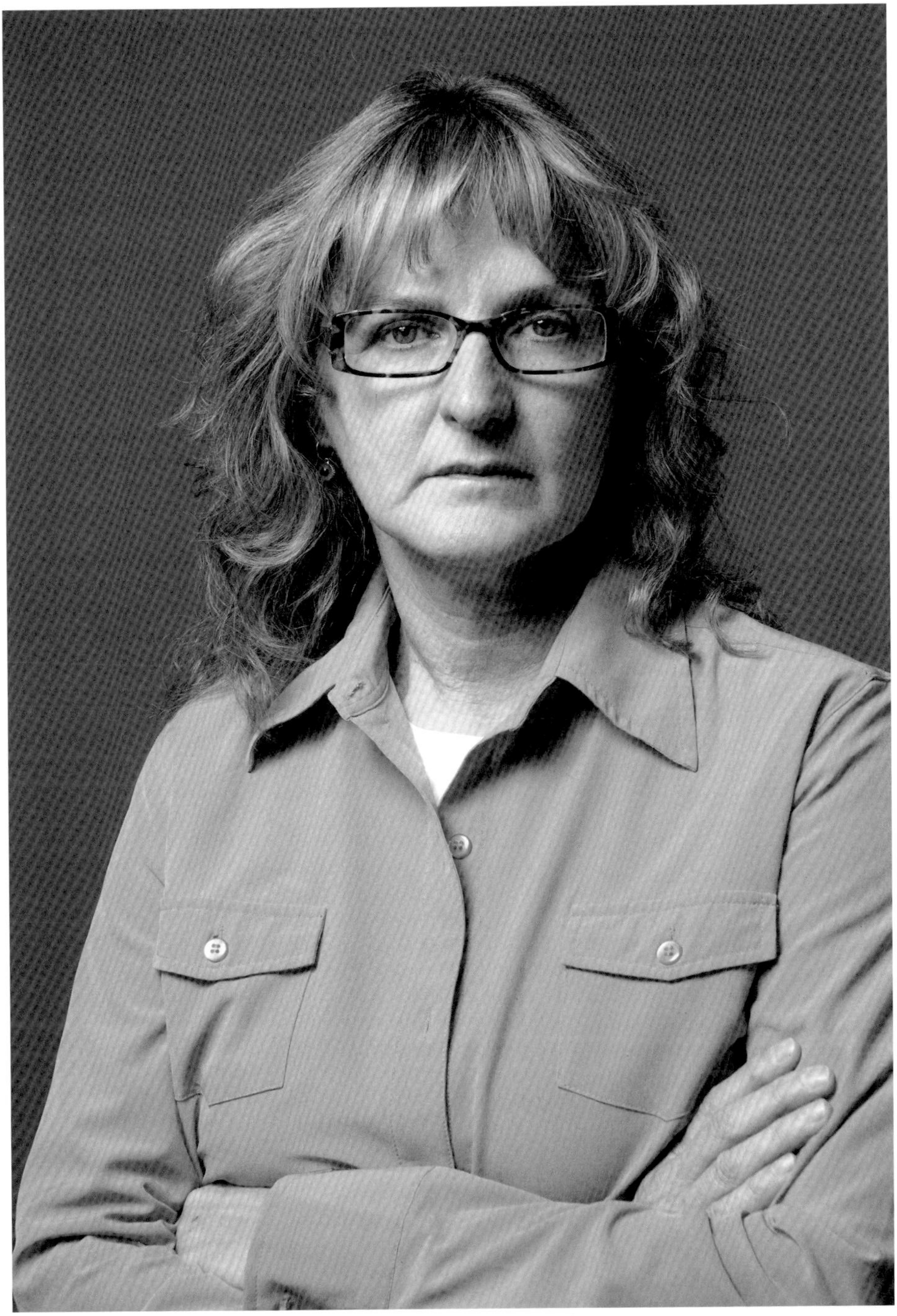

66. *Patti*, 2008

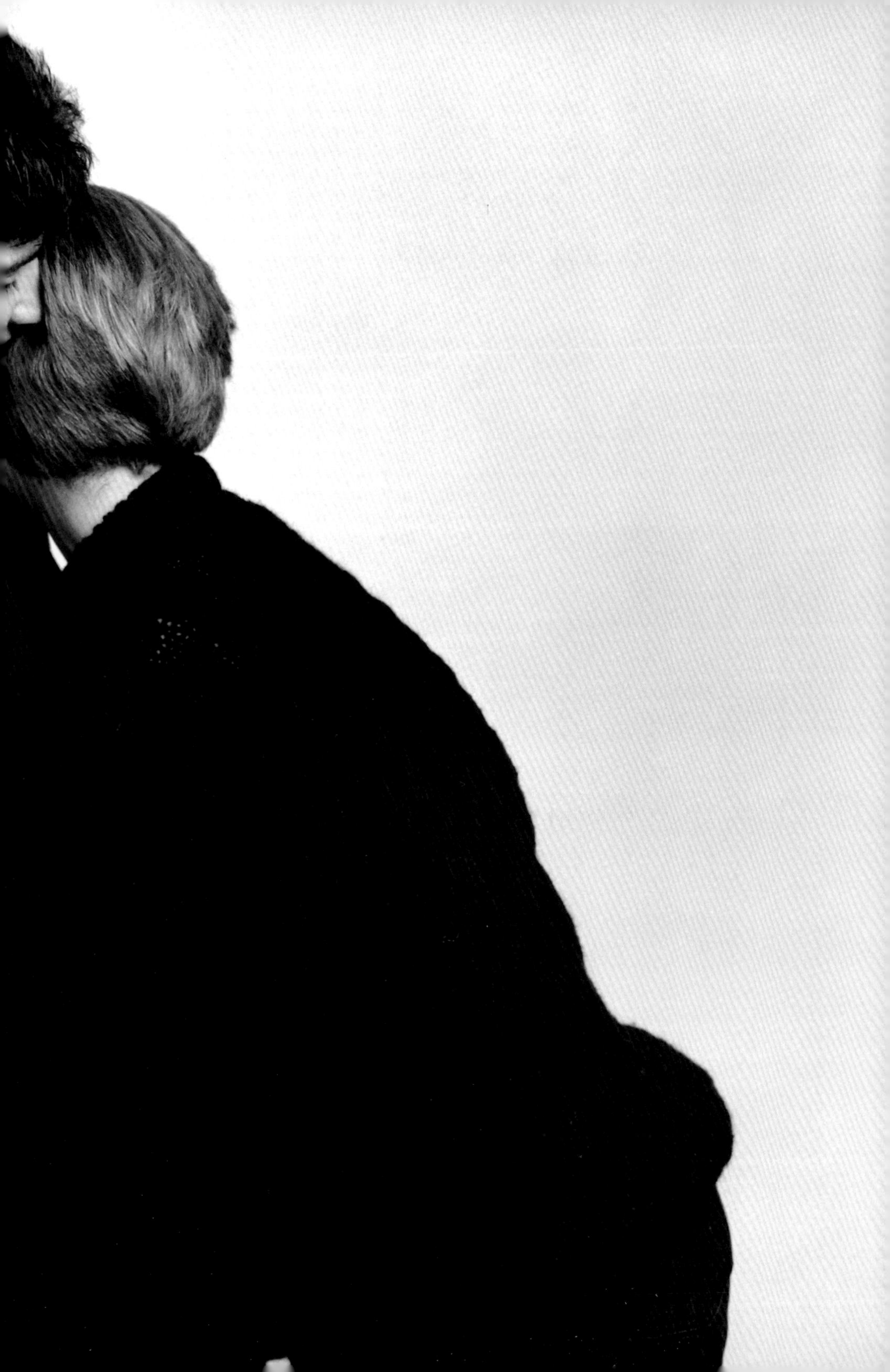

BIOGRAPHY

Sheila Spence is an artist and activist living and working in Winnipeg, Manitoba. Spence's photographs investigate notions of portraiture, self-portraiture, community, and identity. Her portraits have been exhibited locally, nationally, and internationally, and are included in public and corporate collections across Canada. Spence received a diploma in photography in 1977 from Red River College in Winnipeg. From 1989 to 1994 she participated in artist residencies at The Banff Centre, Alberta; the Vu Gallery, Quebec City; and in Newcastle upon Tyne, Manchester, and Liverpool, England. In 1991 Spence partnered with Graham Asmundson to develop the billboard project *Homophobia is Killing Us*. Noreen Stevens joined the project as designer. Afterward Spence and Stevens worked collaboratively under the name Average Good Looks until 1995, creating work about gay and lesbian issues for the public domain. Over the course of her career, Spence has received numerous grants from the Canada Council for the Arts, the Manitoba Arts Council, and the Winnipeg Arts Council. On several occasions she has adjudicated on behalf of the Canada Council for the Arts and the Manitoba Arts Council for various award programs. A tireless volunteer, she has been a governing member on the boards of the following non-profit arts organizations: Floating Gallery, Artspace, CARFAC Manitoba, Mentoring Artists for Women's Art (MAWA), Institute of Contemporary Art and Design, <Site>, St. Norbert Arts and Cultural Centre, and Ace Art. She has twice been a mentor for MAWA (1991–92 and 1995–96). Spence worked at The Winnipeg Art Gallery for almost sixteen years (July 1980 to April 1996) as a staff photographer. She is currently the executive director of the Manitoba Printmakers' Association (Martha Street Studio).

21. *Untitled [Mary and I]*, 1989

EXHIBITION HISTORY

Solo Exhibitions

2008
Pictures of Me, The Winnipeg Art Gallery, Winnipeg, Manitoba

1999–present
Harvest Team, Winnipeg Harvest, Winnipeg, Manitoba

1999
Portrait of a Neighbourhood: Images of West Broadway, Gallery C103, The University of Winnipeg, Winnipeg, Manitoba

1998
Portrait of a Neighbourhood, St. Norbert Arts and Cultural Centre, St. Norbert, Manitoba

1997
Redemption Suite, outdoor installation for the Floating Gallery, *Utopia/Dystopia* festival, Assiniboine River walkway, Winnipeg, Manitoba

1995–97
The faces of dance, on Canadian tour with the Royal Winnipeg Ballet

1994
New Work, Lumiere Gallery, Winnipeg, Manitoba

1992
Points of View, Alliance Française, Winnipeg, Manitoba

1991
De/Constructions, Gallery One One One, School of Art, University of Manitoba, Winnipeg, Manitoba

1990
Portraits in Series, The Photographers Gallery, Saskatoon, Saskatchewan

1989
Portraits in Series, The Floating Gallery, Winnipeg, Manitoba

1988
Portraits of the Human Spirit, The Photographers Gallery, Saskatoon, Saskatchewan

Selected Group Exhibitions

2008
(Re)Visiting the Collection, Gallery C103, The University of Winnipeg, Winnipeg, Manitoba, and on tour throughout Manitoba

2007
Epiphany, Vault Gallery, Winnipeg, Manitoba

2006
Etcetera, Wasagaming Art Centre, Wasagaming, Manitoba

2004
Latitudes, Artget, Academy of Belgrade, Belgrade, Serbia

2004
The Will of Consciousness: Work by Contemporary and Vintage Photographers. Berenice Abbott, Eugene Atget, Lissette Model, Norma Holt, Marian Roth, Sheila Spence, Cherrystone Gallery, Wellfleet, Massachusetts, United States

Portraits in the Collection, Gallery 1C03, The University of Winnipeg, Winnipeg, Manitoba

1997
In Collaboration With, <Site>, Winnipeg, Manitoba

1998
The Light Within, Legislative Building, Winnipeg, Manitoba; on tour throughout Manitoba and to Instituto Cabanas, Guadalajara, Mexico

1996–97
Me, Me, Me and Me, St. Norbert Arts and Cultural Centre, St. Norbert, Manitoba

1994–98
Alliances/The Family, The Canadian Museum of Contemporary Photography, Ottawa, Ontario, toured to Owens Art Gallery, Sackville, New Brunswick; Saint Mary's University Art Gallery, Halifax, Nova Scotia; Nanaimo Art Gallery, Nanaimo, British Columbia; Thunder Bay Art Gallery, Thunder Bay, Ontario; The Mendel Gallery, Saskatoon, Saskatchewan

1993–96
Search, Image and Identity: Voicing our West, Finnish Museum of Art, Helsinki, Finland; Whyte Museum, Banff, Alberta; The Photographers Gallery, Saskatoon, Saskatchewan; STRUTS Gallery, Sackville, New Brunswick; Gallery 44, Toronto, Ontario; Kelowna Art Gallery, Kelowna, British Columbia; The Floating Gallery, Winnipeg, Manitoba

1995
Fractured Spaces, The Winnipeg Art Gallery, Winnipeg, Manitoba

1991
Passionate Regards, Ace Art, Winnipeg, Manitoba

1988–89
Contemporary Canadian Photography (Canada Mexico Exchange) Fotografía Canadiense Contemporanea, Consejo Mexicano De Fotografia, Mexico City, Mexico; toured to Museo De Arte Carrillo Gil, Mexico City, Mexico

1987–88
Multiplicities, Oseredok, Ukrainian Cultural and Education Centre, Winnipeg, Manitoba

1986–87
A Sense of Place, The Winnipeg Art Gallery, Winnipeg, Manitoba

Exhibitions / Public Works by Average Good Looks collective

1995
Here's Looking at You, billboard installation, Peterborough, Ontario

1994–95
Attending to Angels, Cambridge, England

1995
SHE, group exhibition, Lumiere Gallery, Winnipeg, Manitoba

1994
Gays and lesbians. Real family, Newcastle upon Tyne, England

Anti-gay Legislation in Great Britain, outdoor slide presentation, Liverpool, England

Emma's Out.... Feel the Earth Move, poster and postcard, *It's Queer Up North*, Manchester, England

1993
Our Family, Your Family, billboard installation, Winnipeg, Manitoba; Saskatoon and Regina, Saskatchewan; Edmonton and Calgary, Alberta

Touching You. Everyday, Everywhere, pixel board installation, Winnipeg, Manitoba and Calgary, Alberta

1993
Touching You. Everyday, Everywhere, billboard installation, Winnipeg, Manitoba

1992
Passion Pink, group show, Gallery 101, Ottawa, Ontario

Queer Culture Festival, Plug In Gallery, Winnipeg, Manitoba

Lesbian. It's not a dirty word, billboard installation, Winnipeg, Manitoba

1991
Homophobia is Killing Us, billboard installation, Winnipeg, Manitoba

Collections

Air Canada, Winnipeg, Manitoba

Art Gallery of Southwestern Manitoba, Manitoba Arts Council Art Bank, Brandon, Manitoba

Canadian Museum of Contemporary Photography, Ottawa, Ontario

Government of Manitoba Art Collection

Investors Group Corporate Art Collection, Winnipeg, Manitoba

The University of Winnipeg, Winnipeg, Manitoba

The Wellness Centre, Seven Oaks Hospital, Winnipeg, Manitoba

The Winnipeg Art Gallery, Winnipeg, Manitoba

SELECTED BIBLIOGRAPHY

Average Good Looks. "Real Family Emma's Out!" *Locus +* 1993-1996, Samantha Wilkinson, ed. Locus +, Newcastle upon Tyne, 1996: 56–59.

—. *Sub Rosa* (Spring 1994).

—. "Taking Voice: Average Good Looks' Strategies for Facilitating Discourse," in Diana Augaitis et al., ed. *Questions of Community: Artists, Audiences, Coalitions.* Banff, ON: Banff Centre Press, 1995.

Baerwaldt, Wayne. "Fevered Commotion. Gay Activism in the Age of Homophobia." *Border Crossings* 11, 3 (July 1992): 4–9.

Barham, Scott. "Food bank beauty caught." *Winnipeg Free Press* (November 20, 1999): B8.

Canadian Press. "Artist pulls pics of kids from gallery show." *Edmonton Journal* (January 16, 1999): C4.

—. "Mothers protest photos." *Charlottetown Guardian* (January 16, 1999): B7.

DeGrow, Don. "Portrait of a Neighbourhood." *Vitality* (November 1997): 4.

Enright, Robert. "Fictional Lives. The Photograph Portrait of Sheila Spence." *Border Crossings* 6, 1 (December 1986): 44–51.

—. "Border Views. Walk on the Wild Side." *Border Crossings* 17, 3 (July 1998): 6–7.

—. *CBC Heartland* (May 1998).

Frazer, Kelly. "Spence show now an interactive forum." *Perimeter* (January 21 – February 3, 1999): 5.

—."Before the photos came down." *Perimeter* (January 21 – February 3, 1999): 9.

Gibson, Jennifer. *Portrait of a Neighbourhood: Images of West Broadway.* Winnipeg: Gallery 1C03, The University of Winnipeg, 1999.

Investors Group. *The faces of dance.* Winnipeg, MB: Investors Group, 1995.

Karlinsky, Amy. "Sheila Spence on Broadway." *Black/flash* 17, 3 (May 2000): 14–21.

Kelley, Caffyn. "Broken Silence, Visible Wounds: Canadian Artists Explore Social Space With Contradictions Intact." *High Performance* (Los Angeles), #69/70 (Spring/Summer 1995).

Madill, Shirley. *A Sense of Place: Photography in Manitoba.* Winnipeg: The Winnipeg Art Gallery, 1986.

—. "Re/lationships." *Black/flash* 8, 3 (Fall 1990): 14–18.

Marlow, Tammy. "Thieves pilfer photo art." *Winnipeg Sun* (October 2, 1997): 8.

—. "Residents fume over art exhibit." *Winnipeg Sun* (January 13, 1999): 1, 3.

—. "Tempers flare at gallery." *Winnipeg Sun* (January 15, 1999): 3.

Maunder, Mike and Virginia Maracle. "Parents want pictures of children removed." *Winnipeg Free Press* (January 14, 1999): A6.

—. "Art crowd, teens clash over gritty photos." *Winnipeg Free Press* (January 15, 1999): A1–2

—. "Workshop uses art to give kids a voice." *Winnipeg Free Press* (1999): A3.

Perry, Mark. "Child porn ruling is no surprise." *Winnipeg Free Press* (January 19, 1999): 8.

Picard, André. "On home turf in West Broadway." *Globe and Mail* (January 16, 1999): D2.

Scott, Jason. "Bad publicity stresses out city photographer." *Winnipeg Sun* (January 15, 1999): 3.

Simon, Cheryl. "Portraits of the Human Spirit. Photographs of Angela Grauerholz and Sheila Spence." *Blackflash*, 4, 1 (Spring 1988): 12.

Spence, Sheila. "From the Series: Redemption Suite." *Inversions: fairy tales, romance.* Winnipeg, MB: Mentoring Artists for Women's Art (Spring 1997): 38–40.

Stevens, Noreen. "The Chill Factor. Artists Fight Against Unofficial Censorship." *Parallelogramme* 18, 3 (1992–93): 16–18.

Ternette, Nick. "W. Broadway parents clueless." *Winnipeg Sun* (January 28, 1999).

Unknown. "Photo exhibit riles inner-city families." *Winnipeg Free Press* (January 17, 1999): B2.

—. "Art and the truth." *Winnipeg Free Press* (January 18, 1999): A6.

Walker, Morley. "Photo exhibit uproar raises complex issues of class, art, culture." *Winnipeg Free Press* (January 16, 1999): B9.

—. "Controversial photographer unaccustomed to spotlight." *Winnipeg Free Press* (January 16, 1999): B9.

—. "Art lost battle over photo privacy." *Winnipeg Free Press* (January 24, 1999): D1–2.

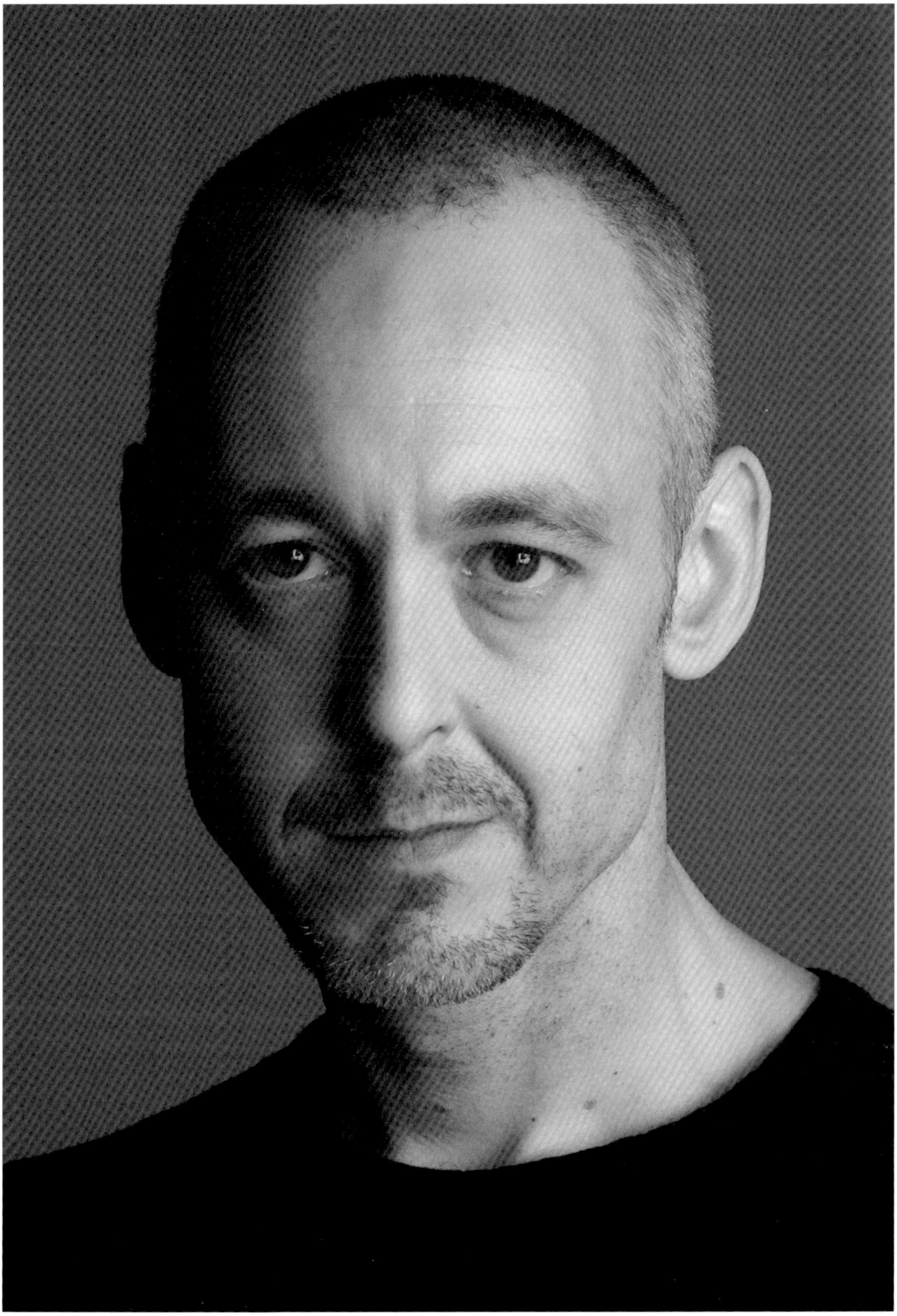

56. *Calvin*, 2007

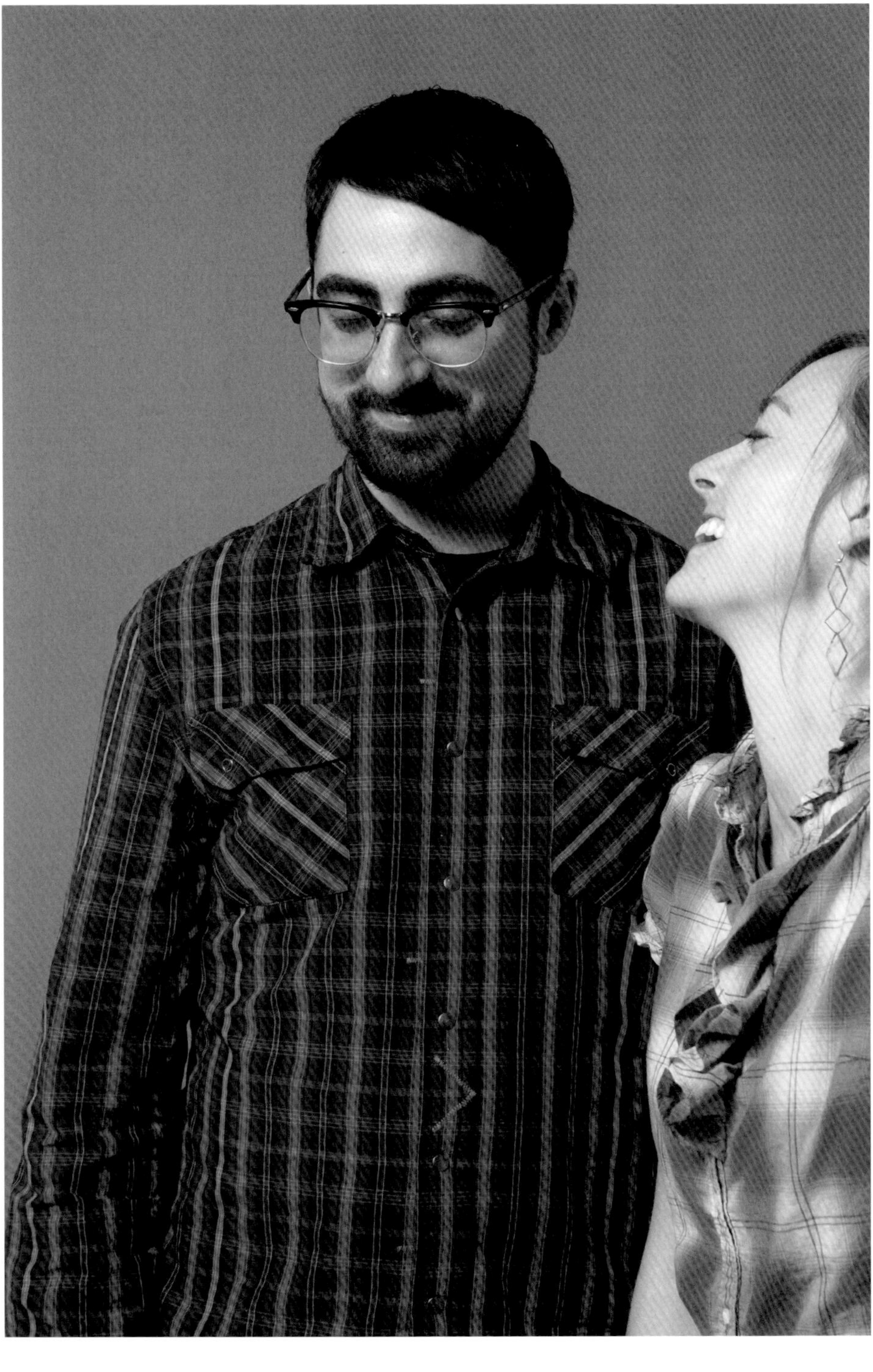

72. *Justin and Suzie*, 2008

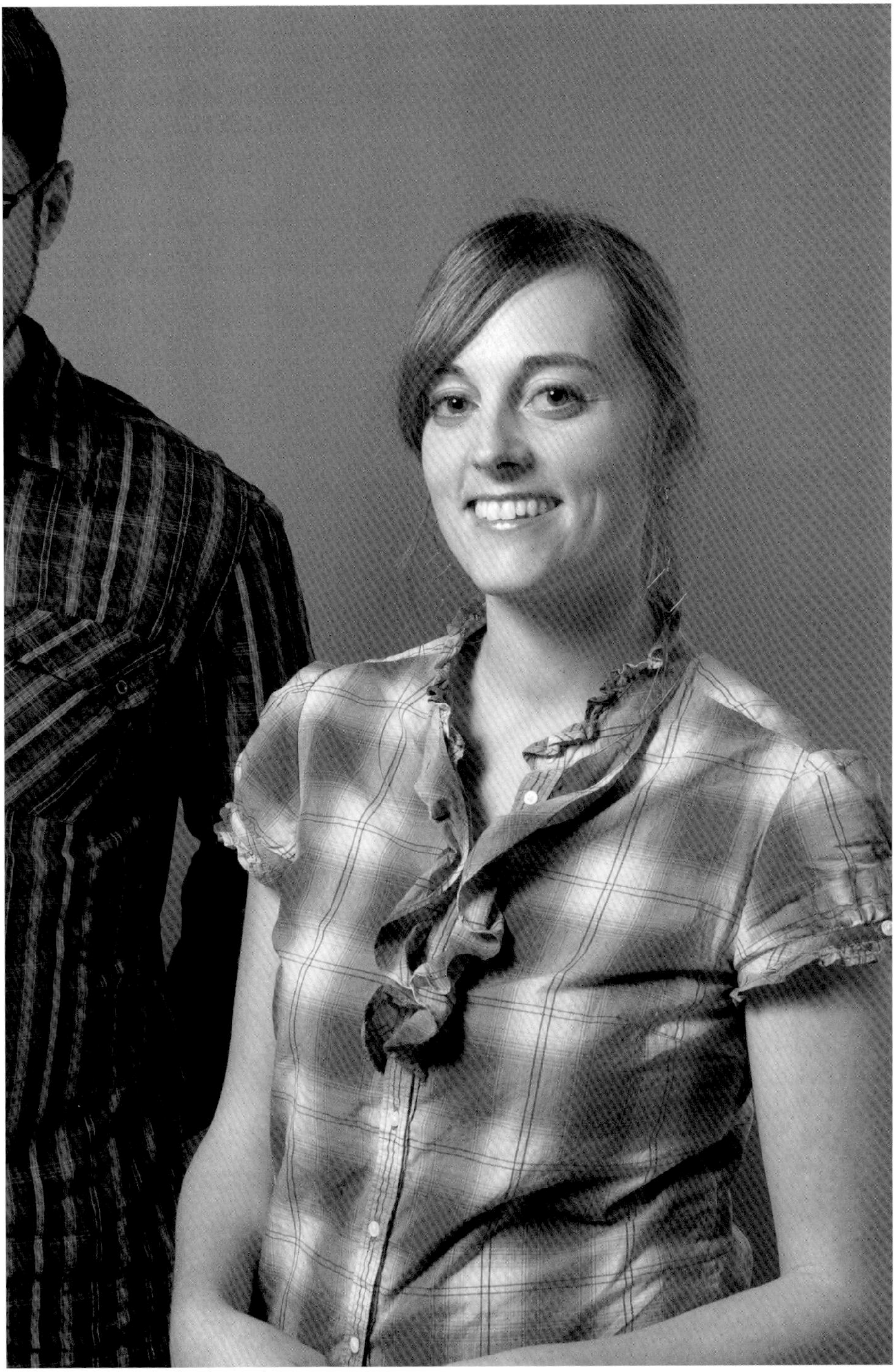

LIST OF WORKS

Dimensions are in centimetres, height x width.
All works are by Sheila Spence. All photography by Sheila Spence.

1
Scott, 1984, silver print on paper, 50.5 x 40.4. Collection of the artist.

2
Roderick, 1985, silver print on paper, 50.5 x 40.4. Collection of the artist.

3
Gerry, 1985, silver print on paper, 50.5 x 40.4. Collection of The Winnipeg Art Gallery; gift of Minolta Canada Ltd., G-87-109.

4
Untitled [Portrait of a Male], 1986, silver print on paper, 50.5 x 40.4. Collection of The Winnipeg Art Gallery; acquired with the Photography Endowment of The Winnipeg Art Gallery Foundation Inc., G-87-89.

5
Nora Smoking, 1986, silver print on paper, 50.5 x 40.4. Collection of The Winnipeg Art Gallery; acquired with the Photography Endowment of The Winnipeg Art Gallery Foundation Inc., G-87-90.

6
Jenny, 1986, silver print on paper, 50.5 x 40.4. Collection of The Winnipeg Art Gallery; acquired with the Photography Endowment of The Winnipeg Art Gallery Foundation Inc., G-87-91.

7
Jordan, 1986, silver print on paper, 50.5 x 40.4. Collection of The University of Winnipeg, Manitoba; gift of the artist.

8
Saul, 1986, silver print on paper, 50.5 x 40.4. Collection of The University of Winnipeg, Manitoba; gift of the artist.

9
Rosalie, 1986, silver print on paper, 50.5 x 40.4. Collection of the artist.

10
Robin, 1986, silver print on paper, 50.5 x 40.4. Collection of the artist.

11
Billy, 1986, silver print on paper, 50.5 x 40.4. Collection of the artist.

12
Nora, 1986, silver print on paper, 50.5 x 40.4. Collection of the artist.

13
Laura, 1986, silver print on paper, 51.0 x 40.5, Collection of the Art Gallery of Southwestern Manitoba, Manitoba Arts Council Art Bank, Brandon, Manitoba.

14
John, Bermuda, 1987, silver print on paper, 50.5 x 40.4. Collection of the artist.

15
Jude, 1988, silver print on paper, 50.5 x 40.4. Collection of the artist.

16
Andrew, Wendy, David, Douglas, and Leone, 1988, silver print on paper, 5 components, 50.5 x 40.4 each. Private collection.

17
Claudette and Margueritte, 1988, silver print on paper, 2 components, 50.5 x 40.4 each. Collection of the Art Gallery of Southwestern Manitoba, Manitoba Arts Council Art Bank, Brandon, Manitoba.

18
Shirley and Kassandra, 1988, silver print on paper, 2 components, 50.5 x 40.4 each. Collection of the Art Gallery of Southwestern Manitoba, Manitoba Arts Council Art Bank, Brandon, Manitoba.

19
Bernadette, Jude, and Katherine, 1988, silver print on paper, 4 components, 50.8 x 40.6 each. Collection of The Winnipeg Art Gallery; acquired with funds from The Winnipeg Art Gallery Foundation Kathleen M. Richardson Fund and with funds from the Canada Council for the Arts Acquisition Assistance program/ Oeuvre achetée avec l'aide du programme d'aide aux acquisitions du Conseil des Arts du Canada, 2007-83. 1 to 4.

20
Sharon and Bob, 1988, silver print on paper, 2 components, 50.8 x 40.6 each. Collection of The Winnipeg Art Gallery; acquired with funds from The Winnipeg Art Gallery Foundation Kathleen M. Richardson Fund and with funds from the Canada Council for the Arts Acquisition Assistance program/Oeuvre achetée avec l'aide du programme d'aide aux acquisitions du Conseil des Arts du Canada, 2007-84. 1 and 2.

21
Untitled [Mary and I], 1989, silver print on paper, 61.0 x 50.8. Collection of the artist.

22
Nancy, Robin, Alison, and Jamie, 1989, silver print on paper, 4 components, 50. 5 x 40.4 each. Collection of the artist.

23
Neal and Tricia, 1989, silver print on paper, 2 components, 50. 5 x 40.4 each. Collection of the artist.

24
Debbie, John, and Stacie, 1989, silver print on paper, 3 components, 50. 5 x 40.4 each. Collection of the artist.

25
Bill and Jean [Dad and Mom], 1989, silver print on paper, 2 components, 50. 5 x 40.4 each. Collection of the artist.

26
Graham and Jamie, 1989, silver print on paper, 4 components, 50. 5 x 40.4 each. Collection of the artist.

27
See Whose Face it Wears [#1], 1989-90, silver print on paper, 61.0 x 50.8. Collection of the artist.

28
See Whose Face it Wears [#3], 1989-90, silver print on paper, 61.0 x 50.8. Collection of the artist.

29
See Whose Face it Wears [#8], 1989-90, silver print on paper, 61.0 x 50.8. Collection of the artist.

30
See Whose Face it Wears [#10], 1989-90, silver print on paper, 61.0 x 50.8. Collection of the artist.

31
See Whose Face it Wears [#11], 1989-90, silver print on paper, 61.0 x 50.8. Collection of the artist.

32
See Whose Face it Wears [#14], 1989-90, silver print on paper, 61.0 x 50.8. Collection of the artist.

33
See Whose Face it Wears [#15], 1989-90, silver print on paper, 61.0 x 50.8. Collection of the artist.

34
See Whose Face it Wears [#16], 1989-90, silver print on paper, 61.0 x 50.8. Collection of the artist.

35
Dream Sequence [1 of 6], 1992, silver print on paper, 111.8 x 50.8. Collection of the artist.

36
Dream Sequence [2 of 6], 1992, silver print on paper, 111.8 x 50.8. Collection of the artist.

37
Dream Sequence [3 of 6], 1992, silver print on paper, 111.8 x 50.8. Collection of the artist.

38
Dream Sequence [4 of 6], 1992, silver print on paper, 111.8 x 50.8. Collection of the artist.

39
Nucking Futs, West Broadway, 1997, silver print on paper, 60.3 x 50.2, Collection of The Winnipeg Art Gallery; gift of the artist, 2007-81.

40
Stephanie, West Broadway, 1997, silver print on paper, 60.3 x 50.2, Collection of The Winnipeg Art Gallery; acquired with funds from The Winnipeg Art Gallery Foundation Kathleen M. Richardson Fund and with funds from the Canada Council for the Arts Acquisition Assistance program/Oeuvre achetée avec l'aide du programme d'aide aux acquisitions du Conseil des Arts du Canada, 2007-85.

41
Stacie and Friends, West Broadway, 1997, silver print on paper, 61.0 x 50.8. Collection of The University of Winnipeg, Manitoba; gift of W.H. & S.E. Loewen.

42
Isaac and Skippy, West Broadway, 1997, silver print on paper, 61.0 x 50.8. Collection of The University of Winnipeg, Manitoba; gift of W.H. & S.E. Loewen.

43
Friday Night Date, West Broadway, 1997, silver print on paper, 61.0 x 50.8. Collection of The University of Winnipeg, Manitoba; gift of W.H. & S.E. Loewen.

44
Ratt Brothers, West Broadway, 1997, silver print on paper, 61.0 x 50.8. Collection of the artist

45
Boy with Wristwatch, West Broadway, 1998, silver print on paper, 61.0 x 50.8. Collection of the artist.

46
Joey, West Broadway, 1997, silver print on paper, 61.0 x 50.8. Collection of the artist.

47
Babysitting Friday Night, West Broadway, 1997, silver print on paper, 61.0 x 50.8. Collection of the artist.

48
Eight, Tray, Deuce, West Broadway, 1998, silver print on paper, 60.3 x 50.2, Collection of The Winnipeg Art Gallery; gift of the artist, 2007-82.

49
19th Birthday, West Broadway, 1998, silver print on paper, 61.0 x 50.8. Collection of the artist.

50
Jennifer, West Broadway, 1998, silver print on paper, 61.0 x 50.8. Collection of the artist.

51
Superman, West Broadway, 1998, silver print on paper, 61.0 x 50.8. Collection of the artist.

52
Timothy, Shane, and Tyrone, West Broadway, 1998, silver print on paper, 61.0 x 50.8. Collection of the artist.

53
Rachel, Tara, and Angel, West Broadway, 1998, silver print on paper, 61.0 x 50.8. Collection of the Investors Group Corporate Art Collection, Winnipeg, Manitoba.

54
Kimberly and Pamela, West Broadway, 1998, silver print on paper, 61.0 x 50.8. Collection of the artist.

55
Parker, 2007, digital pigment on photo rag, 111.7 x 76.0. Collection of the artist.

56
Calvin, 2007, digital pigment on photo rag, 111.7 x 76.0. Collection of the artist.

57
Don, 2007, digital pigment on photo rag, 111.7 x 76.0. Collection of the artist.

58
Suzie, 2007, digital pigment on photo rag, 111.7 x 76.0. Collection of the artist.

59
Andrew, 2007, digital pigment on photo rag, 111.7 x 76.0. Collection of the artist.

60
Ellen and Kate, 2007, digital pigment on photo rag, 2 components, 97.5 x 76.0 each. Collection of the artist.

61
Kim and Sharon, 2007, digital pigment on photo rag, 2 components, 111.7 x 76.0 each. Collection of the artist.

62
Frank, 2008, digital pigment on photo rag, 111.7 x 76.0. Collection of the artist.

63
Claudette, 2008, digital pigment on photo rag, 111.7 x 76.0. Collection of the artist.

64
Bill [Dad], 2008, digital pigment on photo rag, 111.7 x 76.0. Collection of the artist.

65
Wendy, 2008, digital pigment on photo rag, 111.7 x 76.0. Collection of the artist.

66
Patti, 2008, digital pigment on photo rag, 111.7 x 76.0. Collection of the artist.

67
Billy, 2008, digital pigment on photo rag, 111.7 x 76.0. Collection of the artist.

68
Nora, 2008, digital pigment on photo rag, 111.7 x 76.0. Collection of the artist.

69
Graham, 2008, digital pigment on photo rag, 111.7 x 76.0. Collection of the artist.

70
Keith and Eric, 2008, digital pigment on photo rag, 2 components, 111.7 x 76.0 each. Collection of the artist.

71
Stephanie and Marian, 2008, digital pigment on photo rag, 2 components, 111.7 x 76.0 each. Collection of the artist.

72
Justin and Suzie, 2008, digital pigment on photo rag, 2 components, 111.7 x 76.0 each. Collection of the artist.

73
Minnie, Anna, and Amy, 2008, digital pigment on photo rag, 3 components, 111.7 x 76.0 each. Collection of the artist.

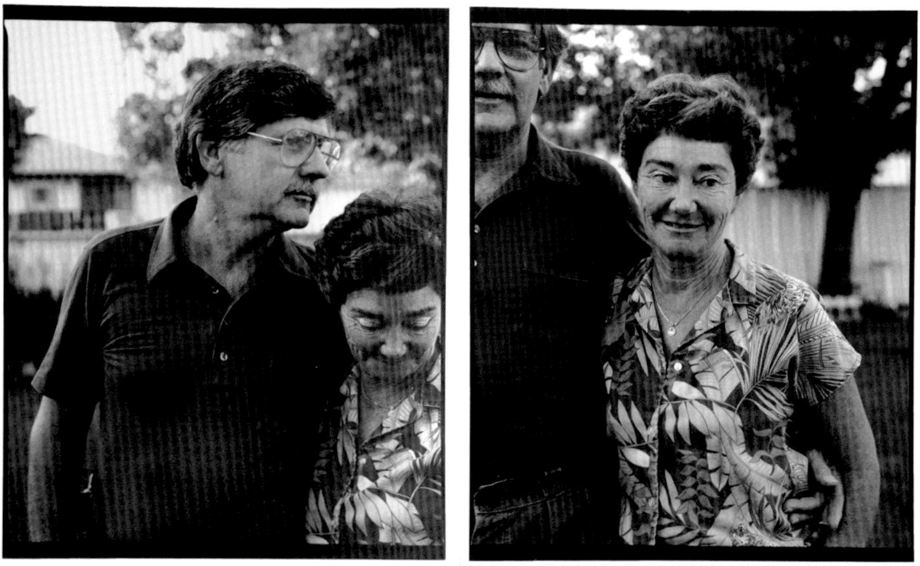

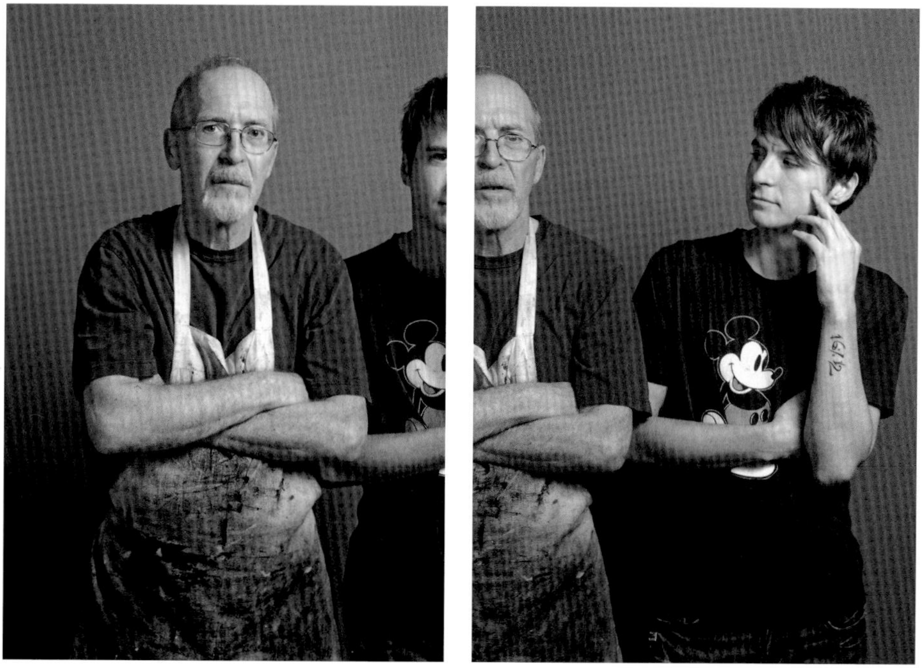

Above 25. *Bill and Jean [Dad and Mom]*, 1989
Below 70. *Keith and Eric*, 2008

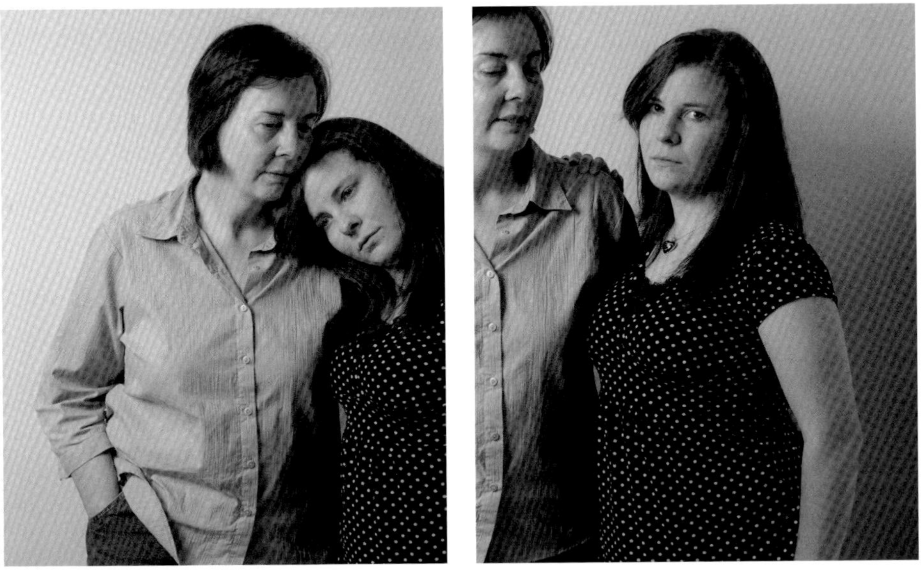

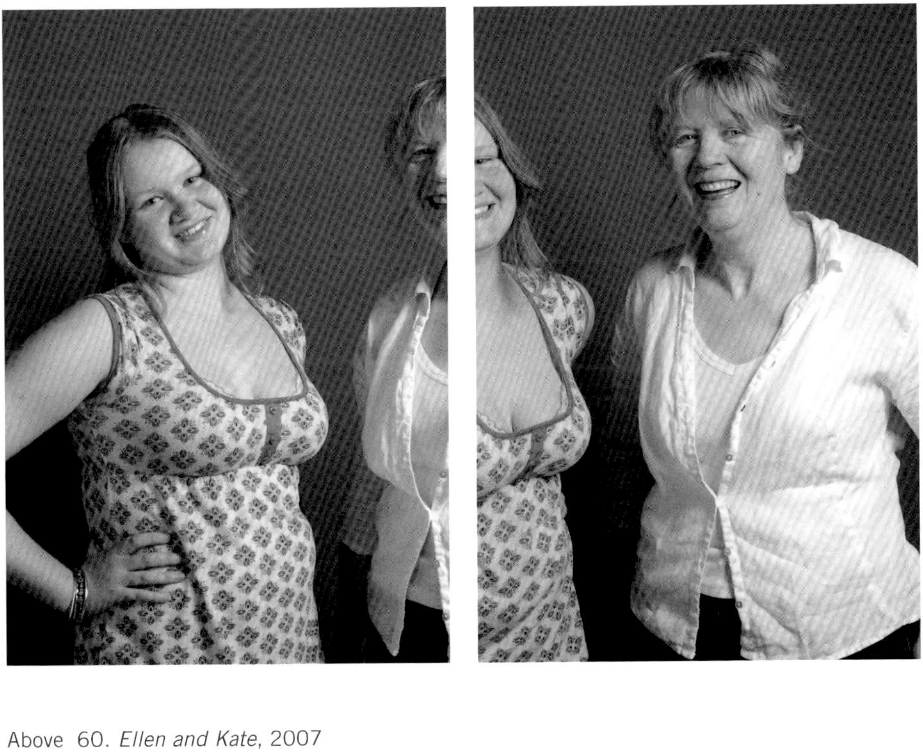

Above 60. *Ellen and Kate*, 2007
Below 71. *Stephanie and Marian*, 2008

ARTIST'S ACKNOWLEDGEMENTS

Patti Jensen, my partner.

Wendy Wilson, my long-time good friend.

All of my friends, family, and colleagues who graciously and generously participated in this lifelong project.

Justin Lee, for his expertise in translating my files into beautiful prints and for his help with my transition to digital photography.

The staff of Martha Street Studio: Suzie, Kristin, Patrick, Andrew, Jeanette, Kevin, and Andrew.

Mary Reid, curator extraordinaire, who has given me the opportunity to exhibit my work in my Winnipeg. Lisa Friesen, designer, for such a beautiful book. The staff at The Winnipeg Art Gallery, for their hard work in mounting this exhibition.

Bob McKaskell. What fun I had!

Marian Butler, for her support and guidance.

The Manitoba Arts Council, for its very generous support for this project and, in fact, my artistic career.

The Winnipeg Arts Council, for its support in getting me started again after a long break.

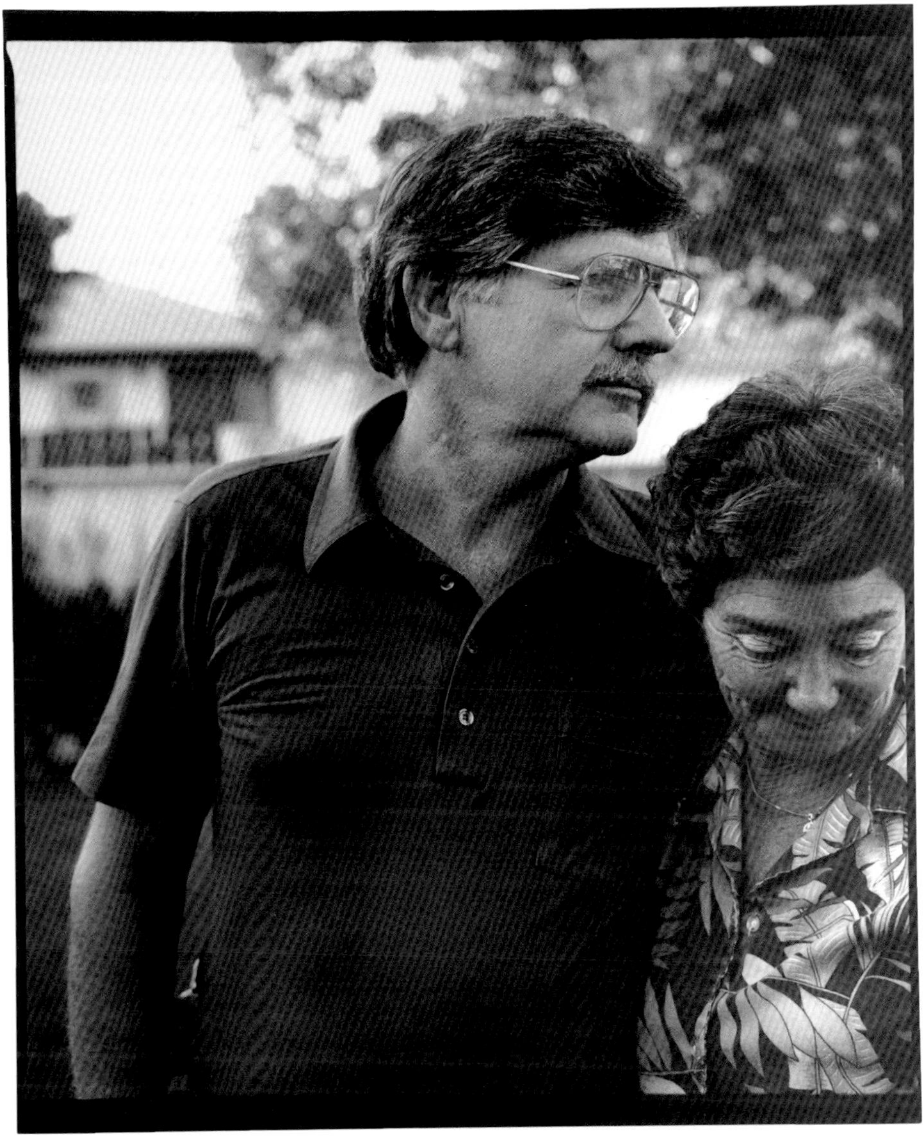

This is dedicated to my mom, Jean Spence.
Mom's strength was drawn from her love for her family and her friends.

25. *Bill and Jean [Dad and Mom]*, 1989 (1 of 2 components)